JOURNEY
to the KINGDOM
Reflections on the Sunday Gospels

by Fr. John Mack

Conciliar Press
Ben Lomond, California

JOURNEY TO THE KINGDOM
Reflections on the Sunday Gospels
© Copyright 2001 by John Mack

All Rights Reserved

Published by   Conciliar Press
                 P.O. Box 76
                 Ben Lomond, California 95005-0076

Printed in the United States of America

ISBN 1-888212-27-6

Unless otherwise noted, all Scripture quotations are from
the New King James Version of the Bible, © 1982
by Thomas Nelson, Inc., Nashville, Tennessee
and are used by permission.

Table of Contents

This book is dedicated to my parents,
Wayne and Carol Mack,
who first instilled in me a deep and abiding love
and respect for the Holy Gospels,
and to my children,
Nathan, David, Jacob, and Michaela,
to whom I hope to give that same love and respect.
I also wish to express my thanks to the many recipients
of my daily e-mail devotionals,
the parish community of Ss. Peter and Paul
Antiochian Mission in Topeka, Kansas,
and to Athanasios and Basiliki Sherry
who labored many hours to make this book possible.

Jan 2007
Fr. John Mack
now a priest in the
Byzantine Catholic Church

chapter 1

Emulating the Mercy of God

Fifteenth Sunday after Pentecost

Luke 6:31–36

"And just as you want men to do to you, you also do to them likewise. But if you love those who love you, what credit is that to you? For even sinners love those who love them. And if you do good to those who do good to you, what credit is that to you? For even sinners do the same. And if you lend to those from whom you hope to receive back, what credit is that to you? For even sinners lend to sinners to receive as much back. But love your enemies, do good, and lend, hoping for nothing in return; and your reward will be great, and you will be sons of the Most High. For He is kind to the unthankful and evil. Therefore be merciful, just as your Father also is merciful."

These words of Jesus are so very straightforward that it is hard to misunderstand them. But our human response is to try to explain them away. How many times do we say, "Well, that might be good in the Church, but it won't work in the real world. If I lend and I don't expect to be paid back, then everyone is going to take advantage of me. You can't run a business or even a household that way. We have to recognize that our Lord is speaking in hyperbole here and He doesn't mean exactly what He says."

We use interpretations like this because we don't like what He says. We don't like this idea that we are to love those who are hateful towards us. We don't like the idea that we are to be kind to those who are rude to us, and we especially don't like the idea that we are supposed to give and expect nothing in return. Yet that is exactly what our Lord says. That is exactly what our Lord expects of us.

If we don't reinterpret His words to mean something other than what they mean, we tend to think of them as applying only in the big sphere of things. We think, "Yeah, if I have a lot, then I'll lend it and I won't expect it back." We tell stories of those who have forgiven murderers and rapists and the like, and think that the requirement to forgive applies only in those situations.

We forget that our Lord is not talking about only the big things. He's talking about those little things that happen to us every day. Someone takes our place while we're standing in a long line at Walmart. Our Lord says that we are to be kind to them; we're not to stand there with that frown on our face and that grumble under our breath, but we are to forgive them. Someone cuts in front of us on the highway, and instead of sitting there fuming with the veins of our neck popping out, or driving quickly and cutting them off, we're to forgive them for what they have done.

Our spouse comes home after a bad day and speaks biting words, and we want to speak back biting words. Our Lord says, "Forgive those who wrong you." Someone asks us to do something for them and we want to say, "Do it for yourself. Why would I do anything nice for you when you've treated me that way?" Our Lord says, "Be kind to those who are rude to you."

Our children ask to use our computers, or to borrow our tools. We know what they're going to do with our computer—they're going to mess it up. And we know that they're going to leave our tools strewn all over the back yard. We want to say, "No, you don't take care of things, you don't follow directions and clean up after yourself, and until you grow up you aren't getting anything from me." And our Lord says, "Lend to those who will not pay you back."

The words of Jesus apply to each one of us in our homes, at work, in our neighborhoods and in our church. We have to face these words. As Christians we are to be different people. Others around us are supposed to know that we are different by our love, our kindness, our generosity. If someone were to talk to our co-workers, would they say that we are kind and loving and generous? If someone were to talk to our children, what would they say about our kindness, love, and generosity? It is sometimes with those we love and those with whom we live that we are the least kind. When we're out in public, we can find it in ourselves to be kind to that person who walks in front of us. But in our homes, just let someone take something they didn't ask for, and there is no kindness then.

We speak to our spouses in ways that we would not speak to anyone else. We speak to our children with that edge in our voice, with that look in our eyes that we would not use with anyone else. Our Lord says, "How can you call yourself My disciple if you are not willing to be merciful to your son or daughter who has just crashed your computer or spilled a glass of orange juice all over the dining room table? How can you call yourself My disciple if you are not willing to forgive the harsh words spoken by your husband or wife?" Be merciful, our Lord says. Be merciful even as your Father in heaven is merciful.

I've talked to many couples, and I've heard this refrain many times when I'm telling someone they need to be loving and to give and to forgive. They say, "I feel like I'm the only one in this relationship who's doing anything. How do you expect me to continue to be loving and kind all the time, if he or she doesn't do anything? He or she just takes and doesn't give. I have to be the merciful, kind, loving and forgiving one. I can't keep doing it unless they give back. I'm running out; I don't have anything else to give. I'm tired."

Be merciful—how?—even as your Father in heaven is merciful. I'll often say to the person who's just said the above to me, "Do you mean to tell me that God hasn't done anything for you, that God hasn't shown any mercy, that God hasn't forgiven you, that God hasn't been kind to you?" They'll look at me and say, "Well, of course. But I want my spouse to be."

I will share with them what our Lord shares with us this morning: We are not to look to others and learn from others how we're supposed to treat them. We're to look to God and the way that God has treated us as the way that we're to treat everyone. Do you see the difference in perspective? People can hate us and be rude to us, but that doesn't give us the right to be rude. The question we need to ask, with anyone in our life, is not, "How does that person treat me?" but, "How does God treat me?"

The day that God is rude to me is the day that I can be rude to somebody else. The day that God is unforgiving to me is the day that I may refuse to forgive someone else. The day that God condemns me is the day that I may condemn someone else. The day that God treats me the way I deserve to be treated is the day that I may treat someone else the way he or she deserves to be treated.

Until that time comes—and it never will come—then I am to treat others the exact same way that God has treated me. If God has forgiven me, then I must forgive them. If God has been kind to me, then I must be kind to them. If God has lent to me, then I must lend to them, asking nothing in return. Even as He has done that for you, then you must do it for your wife and your husband and your friends and your family. "Be merciful, even as your Father in heaven is merciful."

chapter 2

The Sower and the Seed

Seventeenth Sunday after Pentecost
Luke 8:5–15

"A sower went out to sow his seed. And as he sowed, some fell by the wayside; and it was trampled down, and the birds of the air devoured it. Some fell on rock; and as soon as it sprang up, it withered away because it lacked moisture. And some fell among thorns, and the thorns sprang up with it and choked it. But others fell on good ground, sprang up, and yielded a crop a hundredfold." When He had said these things He cried, "He who has ears to hear, let him hear!"

Then His disciples asked Him, saying, "What does this parable mean?" And He said, "To you it has been given to know the mysteries of the kingdom of God, but to the rest it is given in parables, that 'Seeing they may not see, And hearing they may not understand.' Now the parable is this: The seed is the word of God. Those by the wayside are the ones who hear; then the devil comes and takes away the word out of their hearts, lest they should believe and be saved. But the ones on the rock are those who, when they hear, receive the word with joy; and these have no root, who believe for a while and in time of temptation fall away. Now the ones that fell among thorns are those who, when they have heard, go out and are choked with cares, riches, and pleasures of life, and bring no fruit to maturity. But the ones that fell on the good ground are those who, having heard the word with a noble and good heart, keep it and bear fruit with patience."

In this Gospel we are told the parable of the sower, which perhaps would more appropriately be called the parable of the soils.

The sower is our Lord Jesus, and the seed is the Word of God. The soil is the heart of one who hears the Word of God. There are different harvests, because there are different soils, or different kinds of hearts.

There are some hearts that are hardened with their pride and anger, so that they do not listen. Or they may be hardened because they are consumed with the pleasures of this life and have no sensitivity to spiritual things. The hearts that are hard do not even receive the Word of God, so therefore they do not bear any fruit. There is no inclination or movement toward spiritual things, because even as the seed sits in the hardness of their hearts, the devil comes and snatches that Word, lest it should bear fruit.

Then there are hearts that are shallow—the outer part of the heart is able to receive the Word, but the work of repentance has not gone deep. The seed springs forth, but when tribulations come there is no endurance or perseverance. The plant that has grown in the shallow soil of the heart then withers in the heat of the sun and dies.

Jesus also describes a heart that has been plowed, but in which other seeds have been sown. This heart is not vigilant, not united in its search for God, but scattered. Other seeds have been sown in it along with the Word of God. As the Word then springs up and begins to bear fruit, these other seeds also sprout. Jesus describes these seeds as the cares of this life, the pleasures of the flesh. These other seeds grow up and strangle the plant that has been produced by the Word of God, and thus the plant bears no fruit.

Then, Jesus says, there is one other kind of soil. When He speaks to His disciples He describes it as a noble and good heart, a heart that is united in its search for God. The word "noble" here means "single"—not playing games, not devious, not having conflicting goals. This heart receives the Word of God and yields much fruit.

Many things should speak to us from this parable. The most obvious is to look at our hearts and see what kind of heart we have. Do we have a hard heart in which the Word of God sits but cannot penetrate because of our pride, our resentment, our anger, our lust? Do we have a shallow heart, a heart that has been plowed a bit, but on which we have not done the real work of repentance? Do we have a heart that is not watchful, so that many seeds have been sown in it? Or do we have a good and noble heart, a heart that has received the Word of God and is united in the pursuit of God?

We are reminded in this parable that the Word of God, which is thrown out into these various soils, doesn't change. The Fathers say that God's love is for all men, and that God's Word is pronounced to all men. And we see that the Word is life-producing. This is the great encouragement of this parable: we don't have to create the fruit on our own; it is not we who give life to this plant. Our hearts are the soil in which the Word of God grows, but the Word of God is life-giving, and it is the Word of God that produces fruit in our lives.

In the fact that the seed has life and the seed gives life to the plant, we are reminded of the importance of the Word of God. St. Paul says in Colossians 3:16, "Let the Word of Christ dwell in you richly." We are to be those who feed on the Word of God.

Holy Scripture has power; it is the Word of God, and we know that the Word of God is living and active. St. Paul says in Hebrews 4:12, "For the word of God *is* living and powerful, and sharper than any two-edged sword, piercing even to the division of soul and spirit, and of joints and marrow, and is a discerner of the thoughts and intents of the heart." It separates the holy from the profane. It separates that which is honorable to God from that which is dishonorable. St. Athanasius says that the Word of God has life-giving power, and that as we read and meditate on the Word of God and make it our food, the Word itself will inflame our hearts with desire for God.

The Word of God itself will bring us to the point where we hate the things of this world and love the things of God. The Word of God is life-giving and powerful; it produces fruit in our lives. That means that we must be men, women and children who read, study, meditate upon, and memorize the Word of God.

St. John of Kronstadt, in his writings, says that "in the old days" (the old days for him—and remember, he was writing a hundred years ago), when you would go into a pious Orthodox home, you would not hear music of the world. You would hear the music of the Church. If you went into their rooms and looked on the nightstands, you would not find worldly magazines. Instead you would find there the Holy Scriptures. If you looked to see what novels they were reading, you would not find the books of this world, but the lives of the saints. If you sat down to the dinner table, and listened to their conversation, they would not be speaking of the events of this world, but of the events of sacred history. The father would be speaking to his children of Moses and Joshua and Elijah and Jesus and the Holy Apostles. The children would be speaking to each other of the lives of the saints.

He says that in the evening after dinner, if you went to their drawing room, you would hear them reading to each other from the Psalms. They allowed the Word of God to permeate every part of their family's life. St. John then says, "But today, if you go into the homes of the Orthodox, what you hear is exactly what you would hear if you went to the homes of the unbelievers. What they are reading is exactly what the unbelievers are reading." He asks, "Is it any wonder that faith has grown cold? Is it any wonder that we don't see the miracles, the holiness of days gone by, because we have not made the Holy Scripture our own?"

St. John's words are given to us today. When I was a child and my parents would read to me, they never read books from the library. I didn't know what a library was, because what my mother would read at night were the stories from Holy Scripture. When I started to read, I can remember my mother taking the Bible and copying the verses. (I know that she must have simplified it, because it read like, "See Tom run.") The first book I ever read was the Holy Bible.

Each week my father would make us memorize long passages from Holy Scripture. We would look forward to our allowance, which was given on Saturday. In addition to the chores that we had to do throughout the week, we had to recite passages of Holy Scripture in order to receive our allowance. My family believed in the importance of Holy Scripture. When I got older and I was sure that I knew everything there was in the Bible, then they went out and bought me books. The books they bought me were the lives of Christians. Even though I was raised as a Baptist, from the time I was about eight until I was thirteen, I read every single life of a Christian I could get my hands on.

How can we as Orthodox do any less than those who don't have the riches that we have? It is a great tragedy that in many Orthodox homes the children don't know the stories of the Bible or the lives of the saints. We wonder sometimes why our children are not interested in the Church, why they are more interested in the world. It's because they do not hear the Word of God.

We send our children to school and make sure they read all their homework assignments, and we want them to graduate with good grades. We don't show nearly the same amount of interest in their religious education, in making sure that they have read Holy Scripture and made it their own.

St. Seraphim of Sarov used to read all four Gospels every week. St. John of San Francisco had memorized all four Gospels. He didn't want to show everybody that he knew the Gospel readings, so in the Liturgy he would come out holding the Gospel book to read the passage, and somebody would notice that the book was upside down. He never looked at it, because he had not only memorized the Gospels, he had memorized each reading for each day of the year.

These were men who loved the Word of God. We look at their lives and we see such love for God. St. Seraphim of Sarov knelt a thousand days upon a rock in prayer. We think, "Where did he find the energy and the desire to do that?" He had immersed himself in the Word of God, and it bore fruit in his life.

St. John of San Francisco went all day without eating and slept maybe thirty minutes a day, because he couldn't stop praying in his room. He would go to his icon corner and say, "I'll just say a few prayers, and then I'll sit down to sleep," and it would be morning by the time he was done with his prayers. Where did he find that kind of excitement for prayer? He read and memorized Holy Scripture.

St. John Chrysostom, when he would go to his cell at night, before resting would get out the text of Holy Scripture and say, "I need to read just a little bit." His disciple would come in the morning to knock on the door and say, "It's time for prayers, Holy Father," and would hear St. John saying, "I need to read just one more page before I rest." St. John had such love for Holy Scripture that he never read it sitting down. He said, "This is such a holy text that I must read it standing up," and he would stand the entire night, huddled over a shelf built into the wall with a candle, reading page after page of Holy Scripture.

It is said that St. Mark the Ascetic memorized the entire Bible, from the beginning of Genesis to the end of Revelation. When St. Zosimas went out to meet St. Mary of Egypt, she started quoting to him from the Psalms. He said, "Mother, where did you get a Bible?" She said, "Oh, I've never seen a Bible, but the angels have come and taught me the words of Holy Scripture, and I have memorized them."

St. Sergius of Radonezh, as a young boy, had trouble learning to read. He wept and wept because he couldn't read, and he so wanted to read Holy Scripture. Through his prayers the Mother of God granted him the gift of learning, and he immediately ran to the church (not everyone in those days had Bibles in their homes), stood by the reader's stand and began to read Holy Scripture.

In the days of Orthodox England, they would leave the Gospel on the analogion in the middle of the church. The people loved the Word of God so much that the priests had to chain the Gospel book with locks, because people would take it home to read and there would be nothing left. People would come all hours of the night and day so that they might stand and read Holy Scripture.

These are our examples. We are shamed by them. Some of us can't even read the epistle and the Gospel appointed for each day, which takes about three minutes. Days go by and our Bibles sit without being opened. Some of us have never read the entire New Testament. Some of us have never read the Old Testament. Some of us read *TV Guide,* but we don't read the lives of the saints. Some of us watch television every night, and we wouldn't think of missing our favorite show, but it's been months since we read a spiritual book. The examples of our Fathers shame us.

We wonder why we don't have fruit. Why are our lives so empty? Why is it that we have no desire for God? It is because we have not been feeding the fire of love for God. It is because we have not allowed the Word of Christ to dwell in us richly.

As a priest, I long for the day when my people love the Word of God. It gives me great joy when I ask children questions and they know the stories, or when I see little ones acting out the stories read to them by their mothers the night before, because I know that these children will be Orthodox, if we teach them to love the Word of God, if we teach them to love the lives of the saints. We teach them not only with our words, but through the actions of our lives. Those who heard the Word, who received the seeds with a good and noble heart, said Jesus, bore fruit abundantly.

chapter 3

The Hound of Heaven

Eighteenth Sunday after Pentecost
Luke 8:27–39

And when He stepped out on the land, there met Him a certain man from the city who had demons for a long time. And he wore no clothes, nor did he live in a house but in the tombs. When he saw Jesus, he cried out, fell down before Him, and with a loud voice said, "What have I to do with You, Jesus, Son of the Most High God? I beg You, do not torment me!" For He had commanded the unclean spirit to come out of the man. For it had often seized him, and he was kept under guard, bound with chains and shackles; and he broke the bonds and was driven by the demon into the wilderness. Jesus asked him, saying, "What is your name?" And he said, "Legion," because many demons had entered him. And they begged Him that He would not command them to go out into the abyss. Now a herd of many swine was feeding there on the mountain. So they begged Him that He would permit them to enter them. And He permitted them. Then the demons went out of the man and entered the swine, and the herd ran violently down the steep place into the lake and drowned.

When those who fed them saw what had happened, they fled and told it in the city and in the country. Then they went out to see what had happened, and came to Jesus, and found the man from whom the demons had departed, sitting at the feet of Jesus, clothed and in his right mind. And they were afraid. They also who had seen it told them by what means he who had been demon-possessed was healed. Then the whole multitude of the surrounding region of the Gadarenes asked Him to

JOURNEY TO THE KINGDOM

depart from them, for they were seized with great fear. And He got into the boat and returned.

Now the man from whom the demons had departed begged Him that he might be with Him. But Jesus sent him away, saying, "Return to your own house, and tell what great things God has done for you." And he went his way and proclaimed throughout the whole city what great things Jesus had done for him.

Twice in the Church year we are confronted with this Gospel. We read it on the fifth Sunday after Pentecost from the Gospel of St. Matthew—the same account of the demon-possessed men who were living among the Gadarenes (or Gergesenes, as it says in Matthew). Now we hear it from the Gospel of St. Luke, which means that it must be very important.

Let us think about the end of the story, after Jesus has demonstrated His power over the demons, after He has allowed the demons to leave this man and run into the herd of pigs, and send them down over the cliff into the water. Those who were watching the pigs ran and told everyone what Jesus had done. Many came to see what had happened, and when they saw the man sitting there clothed and in his right mind, they were afraid. Then we read these chilling words: they "asked Him to depart from them, for they were seized with great fear."

These people ask the Son of God to leave. They ask God in the flesh, who has come to bring salvation, the Physician of our souls, the Creator of heaven and earth, the Sustainer and Provider for all mankind, Him who rules over all the events and affairs of this life—they ask Him to leave them alone. They would prefer to live without God.

We ask, "How is it that people could ask Jesus to leave? How is it that someone could say to God, 'No, thank You. We don't want You in our lives, in our homes, in our town. We would prefer that You leave us alone. We're fine without You.'" We ask that question because we are concerned for ourselves. We read this text and wonder, "Will we ask Jesus to leave? How can we guard ourselves against making such a tragic mistake as to ask the Son of God to depart?"

Why did they ask Jesus to leave? Jesus has healed this man of his demons and cast them out, and the people have come and seen it. Luke tells us they "asked Him to depart from them, for they were seized with great fear." Fear led them to ask Jesus to depart. We see in this what the Fathers teach us, that fear is a dangerous passion, because fear can lead us to rejecting the Son of God.

Now we ask, "What were these people afraid of?" St. Luke doesn't tell us, but we can guess. They were afraid because God in the flesh had done something new, something unexpected. They were afraid because God had shown to the world their hypocrisy: as many authors have pointed out, what were Jews doing keeping pigs, anyway? Pigs were unclean animals. They were afraid because in that moment of crisis, they saw the difference between God and themselves.

They had been living lives in which they were in control, in which they understood what was going on. Although they were not able to deal with the man who was demon-possessed, they had found a way to live with him out there among the graves. Everything was under their control. They knew what was going to happen, and life was calm. They had a sense of security in the knowledge that things were always the same.

Then Jesus came, and in a day, He changed everything. He turned their world completely upside down. In that miracle He performed, He showed them how empty their world was, how any claim to control they had was simply an illusion. He showed them that He was in control, that He was Lord of the living and the dead, that He was Lord of the elements and of Satan and all his demons. He showed them that He was the ruler of the events of our lives.

They were frightened because they wanted to be in control, they did not want to live by faith. It is a very frightening thing to live by faith, to be dependent on God, because we cannot control God. God had come to control them, and they could not tell this man who had cast the demons out what to do; rather He had come to tell them what to do.

They preferred to live in the shadow of their own control rather than to give themselves over to the control of the Son of God. They preferred to cling to the illusion of self-sufficiency rather than to admit their own weakness and live by faith in the sufficiency of God. So it was easier for them simply to ask God to leave. It was easier for them to remove the person who was shaking up their world than it was for them to face the truth about themselves.

As we look at this story, it is not difficult for us to see ourselves. We so very often do exactly the same thing to God. When God comes into our lives, He makes our lives very uncomfortable. One of the surest signs that God is in our life is that we recognize that we are not in control. We are forced to see all kinds of things about ourselves, to admit our own weakness, and to live with questions that are not answered. We are forced to live moment by moment, depending solely upon God.

It is a fearful place, a place of great anxiety for us if our egos still want to be in control. If we want to find security in knowing everything, in being in control of everything, in knowing exactly how all our needs will be met, exactly how everything will take place, then living with God will be a very frightening experience, because God doesn't tell us what is going to happen tomorrow, or even today. God doesn't answer most of our questions.

And God does not allow us for a minute to think that we have everything covered, because as soon as we begin to feel that way, He allows a crisis to develop somewhere in our lives. Something goes wrong that is unexpected and we must think about our lives. Our lives are filled with these unexpected events. For example, we're busy, we're on a tight budget, and as soon as we go out our car has a flat tire. Things always happen when we least expect them, and at the worst possible time.

God allows these things to happen so that we would be reminded that we need Him, so that we would not seek to control our lives or the lives of those around us, so that we would know freedom—the freedom of faith.

Of course, Satan doesn't want us to know this freedom. Satan wants us to be bound: bound by our own fears, our own anxieties, our desire to be in control and in charge. He presents the way of faith as a way that makes no sense, a way of destruction, a way in which we will lose everything. He seeks to delude us into thinking that our lives would be better without God, so that we would say to God, "Depart. Please leave me alone." Satan does not want us to live by faith.

The possessed man who was healed was the only one who had faith. The villagers say, "Please leave." And the man, in his enthusiasm, says, "Lord, I'd love to go with You," expressing this great faith. "Lord, I want to be with You because You have delivered me." And Jesus turns his world upside-down and says, "No, you can't go with Me." Isn't that just like God? What we expect Him to do, He doesn't do—He does the opposite. To what we think is the perfect request—how can God say no to this one?—He says, "No, I have a different plan for your life."

This man who begged God to stay with Him was given the commission, "No, you go back. You go back to those villagers who didn't want Me to stay and you keep talking about Me." They wanted Jesus to be gone. They wanted to pretend that He hadn't been there. Jesus, in His love for them, says, "They're not gonna get off that easy. I'm not going to listen to them. You go back and you talk every day to every single one of those villagers about what I have done. I want you to be a constant reminder to them of their own pride and ego, a constant voice calling them to faith."

This is what gives us hope. The Fathers refer to God as the Hound of Heaven. Hound dogs are very persistent. Once they have a scent, they don't give up. God is the Hound of Heaven: He will not leave us alone, He will not leave us in this nice world that we have created for ourselves, which is an illusion, a world which will most surely take us to hell. Even if we don't want Him, He will constantly remind us of Himself. The Fathers say that God becomes the burr under the saddle, the rock that's in your shoe when you're hiking that you can't find and you can't get rid of.

God becomes that for all of us, not because He wants to make our lives miserable, but because He loves us. And we get angry. We get angry at God's reminders and at those He commissions to remind us, such as priests and bishops and pious friends. God doesn't pay attention to our anger. God loves us so much that He sends messengers. We can kill the first messenger, and God sends a second. We can kill the second messenger, and God sends a third. We can kill the third messenger, and God will send a fourth, just as He sent prophet after prophet to the children of Israel.

God hounds us with His love until finally He's backed us into a corner and we have nowhere to go. I'm sure you've been in that corner many times, and you break down and say, "Okay, You beat me. I want You in my life. I believe and I will live by faith." You would think we would learn our lesson. But you know what happens—we start getting full of ourselves and we start asking God to leave again. God keeps coming after us until we break and say, "Lord, I believe."

This Gospel lesson ultimately is not about the demon-possessed man nor about the villagers. This Gospel lesson is about Jesus and His love for us. I began by saying that this Gospel lesson frightens me, because I know that I ask God to leave, and I could ask Him to leave my life completely. Yet the Gospel lesson also reassures and comforts me; it reminds me that even if, in my worst moment, I do ask God to leave, God loves me too much to leave me. God desires my salvation too much ever to let me go. God will come again and again.

Those of us who have children worry that our children are going to ask God to leave. It is the greatest fear of my life that, at some point, my child will say, "God, thank You very much, but I don't want You in my life." I don't care what else happens to my children as long as they never live a day without God. Every second of every day I'm praying to God, beseeching God for the salvation of my children.

What a comfort it is for us as parents to know that no matter how our children push God away from them, God will keep going back to them. God will be the Hound of Heaven for our sons and daughters. And how wonderful it is to know that God will not listen to them when they say, "Thank You very much, I don't want You in my life." God will track them down and send messenger after messenger. There will come a point, perhaps, when they won't listen to our voice, but God will send a messenger who will speak. If we pray and if we believe, then at some point God will bring our children back, because God is a God of love, a stubborn God and a patient God. God desires that all men everywhere repent and come to the knowledge of the truth.

So don't despair. Don't give up. Don't listen to your children when they say they don't want to hear any more. You just keep speaking. If it makes them angry, so be it. Just keep speaking to them, because they will not be able to silence your voice forever. At some moment, in the darkness of their own angst, when they're backed into a corner by the love of God, they will be broken by His love and they will repent and say, "Lord, I believe."

chapter 4

Relying on God's Grace

Nineteenth Sunday after Pentecost
Luke 8:41–56

And behold, there came a man named Jairus, and he was a ruler of the synagogue. And he fell down at Jesus' feet and begged Him to come to his house, for he had an only daughter about twelve years of age, and she was dying. But as He went, the multitudes thronged Him. Now a woman, having a flow of blood for twelve years, who had spent all her livelihood on physicians and could not be healed by any, came from behind and touched the border of His garment. And immediately her flow of blood stopped. And Jesus said, "Who touched Me?" When all denied it, Peter and those with him said, "Master, the multitudes throng and press You, and You say, 'Who touched Me?'" But Jesus said, "Somebody touched Me, for I perceived power going out from Me." Now when the woman saw that she was not hidden, she came trembling; and falling down before Him, she declared to Him in the presence of all the people the reason she had touched Him and how she was healed immediately. And He said to her, "Daughter, be of good cheer; your faith has made you well. Go in peace."

While He was still speaking, someone came from the ruler of the synagogue's house, saying to him, "Your daughter is dead. Do not trouble the Teacher." But when Jesus heard it, He answered him, saying, "Do not be afraid; only believe, and she will be made well." When He came into the house, He permitted no one to go in except Peter, James, and John, and the father and mother of the girl. Now all wept and mourned for her; but He said, "Do not weep; she is not dead, but sleeping."

And they ridiculed Him, knowing that she was dead. But He put them all outside, took her by the hand and called, saying, "Little girl, arise." Then her spirit returned, and she arose immediately. And He commanded that she be given something to eat. And her parents were astonished, but He charged them to tell no one what had happened.

This is a very important Gospel, a good reminder to us of certain truths that we sometimes forget in the course of our spiritual lives and of our day-to-day activities. And if we forget them, we forget to our peril.

There are two distinct stories in this Gospel. First is the story of Jairus, whose twelve-year-old daughter is dying. Jairus was a leader of the synagogue. He was a fine man, a respected man, a pious man who kept the commandments. He had every reason to believe that he was among the best of the Jewish race at that time.

Now his twelve-year-old daughter is dying. He comes to Jesus in desperation, with no other option, because there is nothing that anyone can do for her. He asks Jesus if He would come to his house and heal her. Jesus then begins to move. There were many following Him and large crowds surrounding Him. In the crowd was a hidden woman, a woman who was not public like Jairus. Everybody knew Jairus, everybody knew how important he was.

But this woman was different: she was quiet, she was meek, she was hidden. She had been sick for many years. And she had tried all the doctors. No one was able to make her better. In fact, all the doctors just made her worse. She had a flow of blood. In the Old Testament a flow of blood made a woman unclean. A woman who had a flow of blood was not allowed to come into the women's court in the temple. She was not allowed to worship, or to eat of the sacrifices, or to have anything to do with the sacred and the holy. This woman had a perpetual flow of blood. She was cut off from the worship of the people of God.

She comes to Jesus and speaks to Him, not with her words, but with her hands. She reaches out in faith and touches Him, and power goes out of Jesus and she is immediately healed. Jesus stops the crowd and says, "Who touched Me?" She is then brought forward and publicly confesses that she was the one who touched Him. Jesus then publicly says, "Woman, you are healed. Your faith has made you well."

Then the story goes back to Jairus. We are reminded of him because the crowd then reaches Jairus's house. Outside are the crowds of paid mourners who are weeping and wailing and ripping their clothes, anointing their heads with ashes and wearing sackcloth. Jesus tells them to leave. He allows only His three disciples and the mother and father to go in. He speaks to the little girl and says, "Little girl, arise," and she is made completely well.

Now what is the point of these stories? Why is it that the Gospel writer told the two stories together? To understand, we have to think for a minute about the symbolism of what is taking place. Jairus in this story is a type of all the Old Testament believers who kept the law of God as best they could, who used all their energy to pursue and follow after God. His daughter is twelve years old. The number twelve is the number of the tribes in the Old Testament. The faithful of the Old Testament have worked hard to keep the law of God, but they still cannot bring healing. Sickness and death are too strong. This twelve-year-old girl is dying and there is nothing that anyone can do, because all the labors of the pious men and women are not strong enough to defeat death.

So Jairus, at the end of his rope, comes to Jesus and says, "We cannot do it, Lord. We have tried. We have done the best we can, but we cannot do it by ourselves. Lord, come to my house, because Your presence is needed if we are going to have victory over disease and death."

The lesson of that story is that we can never rely upon ourselves. In our Church we talk a great deal about what we are to do. We're supposed to pray, we're supposed to fast, we're supposed to love, we're supposed to withdraw from this sinful world and pursue the heavenly Kingdom. All these laws are given to us—rules and guidelines as to how we are to live. These are necessary.

But sometimes we can err and begin to think that everything depends upon us and that we have to do it all by ourselves. We can either be filled with pride, and think that we are doing it by ourselves, or we can be filled with despair and say, "I can never do it. I can never do enough, and I can never be everything I need to be." It is so easy for us to forget that we can do nothing, unless Christ is dwelling in our hearts.

We are reminded through this story of the words of Jesus, "Without Me you can do nothing" (John 15:5). We are reminded also of the words of the Apostle Paul, "I can do all things through Christ who strengthens me" (Phil. 4:13). Without Christ, all our labors are worthless, because we cannot defeat sin or our passions or the evil one in our own strength. When we invite Christ into the homes of our hearts, then with Christ we can do all things. When we have relied upon His power and done what we must do, not in our own strength, but in the strength which God alone can provide, then even though our efforts are feeble and we make mistakes, it is the power and the presence of Christ that brings healing and victory and salvation.

Now what about this other story, of the woman who had the flow of blood? The significant point of the story is that she has been to every doctor, every possible source of cure. Every doctor has prescribed medicine and it all has failed, because the ways of this world cannot overcome the power of sin and uncleanness. She is healed only when she comes to the end of her self-trust, of trusting in the ways and the wisdom of the world. She is healed only when she is so empty that she can only reach out and touch His garment.

St. John said, "This is the victory that has overcome the world." It's not our brains and our ability to think, not our will and our ability to keep doing the right thing even when it's difficult, not our endurance, not our perseverance, not our stubbornness, though all of those can be good things. "This is the victory that has overcome the world—our faith" (1 John 5:4). The one who overcomes the world is he who believes that Jesus is the Christ, the Son of the Living God.

Jairus could not defeat sin and death with his own power, but he could defeat sin and death by inviting Christ into his home. The woman could not overcome her uncleanness and the stench of her sin by going to doctors of this world. But in one simple gesture, one gesture filled with faith, she received the forgiveness of her sins and the cleansing of her impurity, because it is Christ who heals.

The spiritual life has two parts to it. The part that we talk about a lot is the part of asceticism, of our own labors, of what we must do, because we know that God will not save us unless we do something. Perhaps we talk about it more because we live in a world filled with the false theology of "all you have to do is sit back in a chair and name it and claim it and God does everything." We know that is not true; we must work.

The other side of the spiritual life is grace. We work, but we never, ever think that our works are anything. We work because we must work, but the victory is not found in us. If all we do is look to ourselves, then we will be depressed and discouraged and we will quit, because we know that we cannot win. The victory is Christ's. The victory is the presence and power of God. The victory is grace. As we work in the spiritual life, all the time we are saying, "Lord, come to my house. Lord, come and take up your dwelling in my soul. Lord, give me victory over my sin, because I cannot win this war in my own strength. You are the victor. You are my salvation, my healing and my strength."

Jesus is everything, and we are nothing, our works are nothing. They are as filthy rags, as Isaiah said (cf. Is. 64:6). Christ is the wisdom and power of God. Christ is our salvation. So as we live the Orthodox life, let us make Jesus the center of our very existence. May every beat of our hearts say His name, and may every breath, when we inhale, say, "Lord Jesus Christ, Son of God," and when we exhale may it say, "have mercy on me, a sinner." May we never tire of saying, "Lord Jesus, come."

And Jesus comes when He wants. He comes to bring healing in His own time. So we labor, and in our laboring, we wait. We do not grow discouraged if we have been laboring for a year, or five years, and we see no progress, because we don't expect to see progress until Jesus comes. If we have been laboring for ten, fifteen, twenty years, and the struggle is still as hard, we do not despair because we know that the victory will come in a moment, in the twinkling of an eye.

The victory will come when Jesus says, "Arise." Then we will be healed.

Grace is mysterious. Jesus' coming is not something that we can demand or predict. While our labors are under our control, grace is undeserved and unmerited—grace is grace. Grace is God's. And it never comes because we are worthy. Grace comes because we are needy. Grace comes because we believe. Grace comes because we never stop asking, "Lord Jesus, come."

When grace comes, and the presence of Christ fills the rooms of our hearts, then there is joy. There is joy the likes of which we've never known. Then there is peace, then there is love, then there is victory.

chapter 5

The Prison of Self-Absorption

Twentieth Sunday after Pentecost
Luke 16:19–31

"There was a certain rich man who was clothed in purple and fine linen and fared sumptuously every day. But there was a certain beggar named Lazarus, full of sores, who was laid at his gate, desiring to be fed with the crumbs which fell from the rich man's table. Moreover the dogs came and licked his sores. So it was that the beggar died, and was carried by the angels to Abraham's bosom. The rich man also died and was buried. And being in torments in Hades, he lifted up his eyes and saw Abraham afar off, and Lazarus in his bosom. Then he cried and said, 'Father Abraham, have mercy on me, and send Lazarus that he may dip the tip of his finger in water and cool my tongue; for I am tormented in this flame.' But Abraham said, 'Son, remember that in your lifetime you received your good things, and likewise Lazarus evil things; but now he is comforted and you are tormented. And besides all this, between us and you there is a great gulf fixed, so that those who want to pass from here to you cannot, nor can those from there pass to us.' Then he said, 'I beg you therefore, father, that you would send him to my father's house, for I have five brothers, that he may testify to them, lest they also come to this place of torment.' Abraham said to him, 'They have Moses and the prophets; let them hear them.' And he said, 'No, father Abraham; but if one goes to them from the dead, they will repent.' But he said to him, 'If they do not hear Moses and the prophets, neither will they be persuaded though one rise from the dead.'"

Perhaps the first thing our Lord wants to remind us of in telling this parable is that, no matter how we live—if we live as a beggar sitting by the gates with dogs licking our wounds, or if we live as a rich man who has everything and is well-spoken of by all—there is a common end. All of us must die, and death is the great equalizer. Death comes to all, and we know not when it will come. But death will come for each one of us. And when we die, we leave everything that we have behind.

After death, the rich man and Lazarus were no longer distinguished by their possessions. During this life, you could tell the rich man and Lazarus apart on the basis of the clothes they wore, the food they ate, the houses they lived in (or didn't live in), and the possessions they had. But after death, they were the same. After death, all the distinctions of this life were obliterated, and they were equal before the eyes of God. So we are reminded of the reality of our own death.

We are urged by Jesus to meditate on death, to have death always before us, to remind ourselves each day that this might be the day on which we die. The Fathers say that each night as we go to bed we should see our beds as a coffin, and remind ourselves as we descend into that coffin that we might never rise from it, because each one of us will die. And as Jesus reminds us of the reality of our death—the fact that we cannot buy more time, that when death comes, there is nothing we can do to stop it—we are also reminded that how we live in this life will determine how we experience the life after death.

That is the major lesson of this parable. The rich man lived very well in this world. He would have been envied by most. He had a beautiful house, beautifully adorned and furnished. He had sumptuous meals, drove in a fine chariot, and had many servants. He had many well-wishers and many who spoke well of him. He was a fine, outstanding man in the community, with a position of power and prestige.

The poor man had none of that. He sat at the gates; he didn't even have a roof over his head. He had no one to attend to him, and he was so weakened by his physical disease that he could not even keep the dogs away, as we see in that very pathetic picture, "the dogs came and licked his wounds." And yet, after death, it is the poor man who is residing in Abraham's bosom, and it is the rich man who is enduring the torments of Hades.

As we examine this parable, we ask, "Why? Why is it that the one who lived so poorly in this world enjoys for eternity the blessings of heaven, and the other who lived so sumptuously in this world endures the torments of hell for eternity?" As we look at the parable, we see that there is a correlation between the way these men lived in this world and the way they will spend eternity. The correlation is to be found in the way they viewed themselves and the way they viewed others.

The rich man thought only of himself. Every day he drove by this poor man, this beggar, at his gate. The beggar sat there with rags on his body and no food to eat. And every day, the rich man rode by him and did not stop his carriage. The rich man did not send his servants out with food. He did not send his personal physician out to tend the beggar's wounds. It wasn't that the rich man was mean to him or made his suffering worse. It was rather that the rich man did not see the suffering of Lazarus.

I imagine if you had asked this man, "Is there a beggar who sits by your gates?" he would have thought for a moment, and said to you, "I think . . . yeah, I think there probably is from time to time a beggar who's there." If you had asked him about the beggar's way of life, he would have said, "How do I know how he lives? How do I know if he has any food or what clothes he wears? I don't have time to be taking care of everyone. I'm a busy man. I have many responsibilities. If you're interested in the poor man, go find out yourself. Am I my brother's keeper?"

It wasn't that he was rude. It wasn't that he was mean. It was that he was self-absorbed. He was so busy taking care of himself, dealing with his own problems, that he had no time, interest, or energy to give to the poor man who was sitting by his gates. He lived a self-absorbed life and he died a self-absorbed death. And he spends eternity by himself.

Jesus says when the Son of Man comes and gathers the entire

world to Himself that He will separate the sheep from the goats (cf. Matt. 25:31–46). In that separation, the question will be raised, "How do you tell the difference between a sheep and a goat?" Our Lord will say to the sheep, "When I was sick, you visited Me; when I was hungry, you fed Me; when I was naked, you clothed Me; when I was in prison, you attended to Me. You, who lived your lives caring for Me, come, and I will spend eternity caring for you."

The sheep will say to our Lord, "When did we see You naked and imprisoned? When did we see You hungry? When did we see You sick?" And our Lord will say, "Inasmuch as you did it to the least of these, my brethren. Every time you saw a sick person and took care of him, every time you saw someone who had nothing, and gave to him of what you had, then you took care of Me. And inasmuch as you have lived your life taking care of others, inasmuch as you have lived your life with love for your fellow man, then you are able to receive My love. You are able to be with Me because I am filled with love for all mankind. I spent My life taking care of the needy, the poor, the beggars, the lame, the deaf, and the dumb. And inasmuch as you have lived like Me, then we will spend eternity together."

The goats will say, "Lord, we don't understand. If we had seen You, we would have taken care of You, but we didn't see You. When did we see You naked, and didn't clothe You? When did we see You hungry, and didn't feed You? When did we see You poor, and a beggar, and at our gates, and we didn't stop our carriage to take care of You?" And our Lord will say to them, "That's exactly the point that I'm making: you didn't see Me, because you didn't look for Me. Because you spent your life taking care of yourself and you had no concern for others. Because you are self-absorbed. And because you are full of yourself, there is no room in you for Me. And as much as I would love to gather you and take you to be with Me, you cannot receive My love, because you do not love those who are in need. Because you are so self-absorbed, you can only know your own love. And you must live for eternity with the pain and agony of loving only yourself."

The poor man, Lazarus—who had an awful life, a life that no

one would want—lived his life not concerned about himself. He lived his life open in concern for others. It's an amazing thing: this poor man every day saw this rich man go by, but he did not become angry. Most of us, if we were sitting at the gates of a rich man's house, living with no food and with rags on our bodies and open sores, would become bitter and angry and resentful of this rich man. We would become bitter and angry at God. We would say to God, "How come You set life up like this? Why is it that some have too much and some have too little? And how come I'm the one who has too little? Hey, life isn't fair."

The poor man sitting at the gates never once questioned God, never once was bitter, or angry, or resentful against the rich man, because he wasn't self-absorbed. This poor man had joy in the rich man's prosperity. He gave thanks to God that the rich man had health while he had sickness. He gave thanks to God that the rich man had food while he had nothing to eat. He gave thanks to God that the rich man lived in prosperity while he himself had nothing. It is because he lived life without concern for himself that, when he died, the angels came and took his soul. That is a beautiful and a fearful picture, because we are told that the rich man died and there were no angels to take his soul. There were only demons to drag him down to the pit of hell.

How we live will determine how we spend eternity. If we live for ourselves, if we are so absorbed in ourselves that we cannot cry for anyone else, that we don't even see the beggars, the poor, the needy, that if they ask us for help we take it as an insult, that we see ourselves as being better than others and deserving more than others, that we can feast sumptuously while there are people who have nothing to eat—then we will not be able to receive the love of God. God will look at us and see nothing in us that reminds Him of Himself, because God could not stand to see us living in poverty while He was living in riches. He made Himself poor and became one of us, the poor ones, so that He might exalt us. And it is only those who are like God who will enjoy being with God for eternity.

At the end of the parable, the rich man says, "Send Lazarus back to my brothers, so that they will repent." And Abraham says,

"If I sent Lazarus back, it would do no good. Even if they saw one risen from the dead, they would not repent because they are so self-absorbed that they cannot be taught. They cannot see the truth that is in front of them. If they will not listen to the Law and the Prophets, then they will not listen even if one is raised from the dead."

This is a fearsome parable, one that should cause us to look deeply into our own souls. It should motivate us to look for the beggars at our gates. It should speak to us that we fare sumptuously every day while others are starving, and we do not care. All our religious talk and activity means nothing if our hearts do not break for the poor, and the lonely, and the oppressed. It means absolutely nothing if we care only for ourselves.

It is far better to live as a Lazarus than to live as a rich man. It is far better to live with nothing than it is to live with everything, because things have a way of deadening our hearts. Full meals have a way of making us insensitive. It is those who are hungry who care about those who are hungry, whereas those who are full care only for themselves.

So we must voluntarily choose poverty. We must voluntarily choose emptiness. We must voluntarily choose a meager meal, so that our hearts remain soft, so that we can see a picture of a boy whose belly is distended because he has no food, and we will weep. Even if we see a thousand pictures, we will shed thousands of tears, because our hearts have been made soft.

The Fathers say that there is a third truth to be found in this parable: only those who suffer know how to love. Those who avoid all suffering, those who live with plenty, may speak words of love, but they do not know the reality of love. True love is planted and grows in the heart of one who suffers.

How different the eyes of eternity are. Everyone in that town looked at Lazarus and said, "What a poor and disgusting man. What an awful way to live." And everyone looked at the rich man and said, "Oh, I want to be like him." As they raised their children and walked by the house, they said, "Now, look at Lazarus; don't you grow up to be like him. Don't you grow up to sit in a rich man's gate. You grow up to be like the man who owns that house. You work hard at school. You go on to college, and you get a good degree, and you work hard, and you can be like that rich man someday. We believe in you. You can do it."

From the eyes of eternity, the angels walked by and said, "You see that man, Lazarus. Be like him. You be like that man in the gate, with the sores, because his heart is open." And those same angels whispered in the ears of all those who were attendant to the whispering of the angels, "You see that rich man. Whatever you do, don't be like him, because his heart is closed. God has given him enough that he could build a mansion in paradise. He could share with thousands of beggars. He could open wide the gates of heaven through his almsgiving, but he only cares about himself. The gates that he builds are for himself, and the barns that he builds are for himself, and he has built nothing for himself in paradise."

We need to write this parable in our hearts. If you let this parable sink deep into your soul, then you'll be a very different person than you are today. And we have just a few years left. Then all of us will be dead. It'll be too late then to share with those who need, because we'll be locked in the prison of our own self-love.

Some of the Fathers were asked to describe hell, and one Father said this (and I think it is the best description of hell I've ever heard): "Hell is to be locked, naked, in a room full of mirrors for eternity." Some of us are building that room for ourselves, because some of us only look at ourselves, and only ask, "What do I need?" and "What do I want?" and "How do I look?" and "What is going to happen to my future?" Each week we live that way, we construct a new mirror, and we shorten the opening through which we might escape.

Let us begin to ask, instead, "What do they need?" Let us ask of our spouse, "What does he or she want?" of our children, "What is best for them?" and of those who live in this world, "What can I give?" With the words and the actions of charity, we can destroy the mirrors that imprison us, so that when we die the angels may gather our souls, and we will dwell in the bosom of Abraham.

chapter 6

The Good Samaritan

Twenty-first Sunday after Pentecost
Luke 10:25–37

And behold, a certain lawyer stood up and tested Him, saying, "Teacher, what shall I do to inherit eternal life?" He said to him, "What is written in the law? What is your reading of it?" So he answered and said, "'You shall love the LORD your God with all your heart, with all your soul, with all your strength, and with all your mind,' and 'your neighbor as yourself.'" And He said to him, "You have answered rightly; do this and you will live." But he, wanting to justify himself, said to Jesus, "And who is my neighbor?"

Then Jesus answered and said: "A certain man went down from Jerusalem to Jericho, and fell among thieves, who stripped him of his clothing, wounded him, and departed, leaving him half dead. Now by chance a certain priest came down that road. And when he saw him, he passed by on the other side. Likewise a Levite, when he arrived at the place, came and looked, and passed by on the other side. But a certain Samaritan, as he journeyed, came where he was. And when he saw him, he had compassion. So he went to him and bandaged his wounds, pouring on oil and wine; and he set him on his own animal, brought him to an inn, and took care of him. On the next day, when he departed, he took out two denarii, gave them to the innkeeper, and said to him, 'Take care of him; and whatever more you spend, when I come again, I will repay you.' So which of these three do you think was neighbor to him who fell among the thieves?" And he said, "He who showed mercy on him." Then Jesus said to him, "Go and do likewise."

In this Gospel lesson we hear the very familiar story of the Good Samaritan. Every year we read it when we are beginning to prepare ourselves for the celebration of the Nativity of our Lord.

We are preparing ourselves to remember the wonderful message that our Lord, the second Person of the Godhead who existed from all eternity, looked down on us in our poverty and sin and depravity and wretchedness, and He did not stay in heaven, keeping all His riches and goodness and love for Himself, but He willingly gave. He emptied Himself, to use the words of St. Paul in Philippians 2. He who was rich, for our sakes became poor, to use the image of St. Paul in 2 Corinthians 8, that we through His poverty might be made rich.

During the Nativity Fast we begin to meditate upon this unbelievable truth, this truth that has changed our lives and history—that from a pure Virgin, God became man. As we meditate upon this truth, we ask, how do we prepare ourselves to celebrate the Nativity of our Lord?

Certainly, we prepare ourselves, as in any fast season, by fasting and prayer, which help us to repent. But there is something else that we must do. Every fast has three components: we fast, we pray, and we give alms. If there is any fast of the Church year that is specifically dedicated to this third, it is the Nativity Fast. We remember, in the Feast of the Nativity, the almsgiving of God. We remember that God gave everything—He gave Himself—so that we in our poverty might be made rich. If we are going to receive this message with joy, then we must live like God: we must empty ourselves so that others may be made rich.

This is the message of the parable of the Good Samaritan. At the very end, when Jesus had spoken of the Samaritan who gave of his time and money to help this poor Jew who had been robbed, He said, "Go and do likewise." We are to live the same way the Good Samaritan lived, because we know that the Good Samaritan is none other than Jesus Christ Himself. How can we call ourselves the followers of Christ if we do not give generously to those who are in need?

Just a few days before the Advent Fast, we commemorate our

Holy Father John the Almsgiver. I love his story. When he was a boy, twelve years old, he was sleeping one night, and he had a vision. As he describes the vision in his autobiography, he saw a beautiful young maiden standing at the foot of his bed. He sat up and shook himself and rubbed his eyes several times, but she didn't go away. He looked at this beautiful young woman and asked, "Who are you and why are you here?"

She said to him, "I have come because I am the one who opens the door of paradise. John, as you grow older, if you want to enter paradise, then you must take me to be your bride. You must follow me and live with me, because I am the door to paradise. If you make me your bride, then when you die the gates of paradise will open wide and God will receive you in glory."

John looked at her and said, "But who are you? What is your name?" She said, "My name will become known to you, but I will tell you this—I am the one who caused the birth of Christ." With that she disappeared.

John thought for a minute, and he realized that her name was Compassion, because it was compassion that brought God to earth and that opens the doors of paradise to us. St. John dedicated himself to living a life of compassion. Years later, when he was elevated to the patriarchal throne of Alexandria, he called his servants to him and said, "I want you to go throughout this town and write down the names of all of my lords. I know that I have many bosses, and I want you to write their names down and bring the list back to me."

His servants looked at him with a bit of surprise and confusion. "You're the patriarch—what do you mean, your bosses, your lords? When you become patriarch, that means you're the boss of them. Who are your lords?"

He said, "You go out and find every beggar and every poor person, and you write their names down, because they are my lords." His servants walked through the town of Alexandria, and they wrote down the names of 7,500 people who were living in shacks and on street corners, and who did not have enough to eat. They brought this list back to John.

John said, "Now you must use all that I have inherited as

patriarch to serve these, my lords." He commanded that the poor be fed out of the treasury. He himself went out during the day and looked for the poor. It was noised abroad that the Patriarch of Alexandria was very different, that he would give to all. People flocked to the city of Alexandria.

Among the people were some who were not truly poor, who saw in St. John an opportunity to get rich quick through the work of others. There was one particular man who dressed up as a beggar in torn clothing. John had the habit of giving out six gold pieces to every person he met who was poor. So this beggar came up to him and said, "I'm poor, I don't have enough to eat."

The servants looked at him and John said, "Give him the six pieces." They gave him six pieces, and the man pocketed them and ran around the corner, put on a different beggar's outfit, and came running back to John. He said, "I'm a beggar, I need money." John said, "Give it to him." The servants looked at him and said, "He was here just a few minutes ago, we've seen him before."

John said, "Is there something wrong with my communication? I said give him the gold." They gave him the six pieces of gold. The beggar pocketed them and ran and changed his clothes again. He came running back to John and said, "I'm poor, I'm in need." The servants were beside themselves. They looked at St. John and said, "Don't you understand, you're being had. This man is using you. He's already gotten twelve—are you going to give him more?"

St. John said, "This time give him twelve gold pieces, because his name is Jesus, and He is testing me to see whether I am truly compassionate." He gave that man twelve gold pieces. St. John was a Good Samaritan, because he said many times, "It is not my place to judge. It is not my place to say who is worthy and who is unworthy. If God had used that method of deciding who would receive His grace and who would not, then I never would have received His grace, because I was the most unworthy. And yet when Jesus was born, He gave Himself for all of humanity, for the worthy and the unworthy. How can I, who celebrate His Nativity, do anything else?"

The words of Jesus, "Go and do likewise," mean exactly what they say. When we see someone who is needy, then we must give.

We must give even if we have little. We must give away even all that we have. You know how our conniving, logical mind enters in and wants to make deals—to do what God says and yet take care of ourselves.

The story is told in St. John's Life that eventually there was very little gold left in the treasury. St. John was so merciful that he would take the possessions of the Church and melt them down so that he would have gold to give away. He would take his episcopal vestments and have them cut up and made into clothing when he ran out of money. Finally, they had only fifteen gold pieces in the entire treasury. His servants got together and used that calculating machine, which is our ego and our mind, and talked among themselves.

They said, "You know, this patriarch doesn't understand money. We've got a responsibility to this patriarchate. We have to preserve it. If he gives everything away, there'll be nothing left for the next patriarch. So we have to use wisdom and conniving. Let's agree among ourselves that we'll tell him that we're doing what he says, but we're going to have to save some of this money and invest it so that we have money left over after he dies. We can't let him give away everything."

At that moment St. John came in and said, "There's a poor man here and I want you to give him fifteen gold pieces." The servants said, "Yes." They winked at each other and after he left they walked out and gave the man five gold pieces instead of fifteen. They said, "You know, we can do this all the time. We can give a little so they won't come back and complain, and still preserve a little bit for ourselves."

St. John knew what they had done, because you can't hide anything from the saints. They see through it. That afternoon a woman came and gave him five hundred pounds of gold. St. John knew, because it was revealed to him, that she had intended to give them more, but she had only given five hundred. So he called the servants in and said to the lady, "How much did you intend to give?"

She said, "I intended to give fifteen hundred pounds of gold, but this morning, when I got up, and I had the note for the bank on which I'd written 'one thousand, five hundred,' the 'one thousand' had been erased, and there was only 'five hundred' left. I knew that God only wanted me to give five hundred."

St. John turned to the servants and said, "See? I told you to give fifteen, and you gave five. God told her, instead of giving us fifteen hundred, to give us five hundred. Do you see how your logical, conniving brain has stolen from the Church, because you thought that you could take better care of it than God could?" From that day on, the servants gave away everything that St. John told them to give, and there was always enough, because God will take care of those who give.

This Advent is given to us to learn this truth. Unfortunately, Christmas comes and every year we spend more on ourselves than we do on anyone else. We spend massive amounts on our children, who don't need anything, while there are children in Calcutta who are starving. We give gifts to each other, when we should be using that money for the poor.

Every year the Holy Church reminds us of these truths. One of these years we have to follow, we have to obey, we have to make compassion our bride. Jesus said, "If you do good to those who do good back to you, what credit is that to you?" Even the ungodly this Christmas are going to give presents to their friends. That's the way the world works: you give presents to those who can give presents back to you. Jesus says, "What good is that? I say to you, give presents to those who will not receive presents. Give food to those who have no food" (cf. Luke 6:27–36).

There are many reasons for fasting. We fast to exercise self-control. We fast so that we might remember that Jesus is the heavenly bread, and men cannot live by bread alone, but by every word that comes from the mouth of God. But we also fast so that we might have more to give away. There's something tragically wrong when we spend more money on food during fasting times than we do outside of the fast. We obscure and lose one of the reasons that we fast.

It would be far better for us periodically throughout this Advent to sit down to a dinner of bread, so that we can give to someone else who never has a four-course dinner. It would be very good for us this Lent to drink only water so that we might be able to send money to Calcutta so that children who have nothing may be fed.

You see, Jesus gave everything. Jesus was rich and for our sakes He became poor. Almost everyone in America is rich, because we are among the world's richest five percent. How can we live lives that are centered on ourselves, when ninety-five percent of the world is very poor in comparison to us? It's going to go hard for Americans on the Day of Judgment. I warn you: Americans who are fat, who have everything they need, are going to be standing before the judgment seat of God with children who died of starvation. God is going to require of us their starvation.

One time a man brought St. John a very fancy blanket, because he was worried. He had seen what the patriarch was sleeping on. He thought, "That's no way for a patriarch to sleep. He needs a fancy, rich blanket." He gave it to St. John, who thought, "You know, this man has bought this for me and I really should sleep on it." So he lay down to sleep with this very rich, down-filled blanket. He woke up in the middle of the night in absolute terror. He sat up in his bed and said, "How can I sleep with this blanket, when right now on the streets of this city there are children who have no blanket? They're shivering in the cold! How can I enjoy this while many of my flock have no house? Many of them have no beds."

In the morning he got up and marched to the market. He took the beautiful blanket and sold it. With the money he bought several ordinary blankets and distributed them to the poor. The rich man came to the market the next morning and said, "That looks like the blanket I gave to the patriarch! I know what he did! Why? Patriarchs need to sleep under good blankets." He bought it again and he gave it to John.

John went back and sold it again and gave away more blankets to the poor. The rich man went back the next morning and bought it again. This lasted about a week until finally John wrote to him, "Let's keep this up. This is wonderful! Let's see who wins, let's see who's more stubborn, I who give it away or you who keep buying it."

St. John had made compassion his bride. He was a compassionate person; he was a Good Samaritan. And when he died, the angels came for his soul. On the Day of Judgment there aren't going to be starving children who accuse him; there are going to be children with beautiful clothes who speak well of him. There are going to be poor people who stand beside him and say, "This man fed me, this man clothed me, this man visited me when I was in prison, this man took care of me when I was sick." And the Lord will say to him, "Inasmuch as you did it to one of the least of my children, you did it unto Me."

chapter 7

Being Rich Toward God

Twenty-second Sunday after Pentecost
Luke 12:16–21

Then He spoke a parable to them, saying: "The ground of a certain rich man yielded plentifully. And he thought within himself, saying, 'What shall I do, since I have no room to store my crops?' So he said, 'I will do this: I will pull down my barns and build greater, and there I will store all my crops and my goods. And I will say to my soul, "Soul, you have many goods laid up for many years; take your ease; eat, drink, and be merry."' But God said to him, 'Fool! This night your soul will be required of you; then whose will those things be which you have provided?' So is he who lays up treasure for himself, and is not rich toward God."

There is an obvious lesson in this Gospel, which continues the Church's Advent theme of generosity. What did this rich man do wrong? We can see two mistakes that the rich man made and that you and I could make. You can make these same mistakes whether you have many things or few.

The first mistake the rich man made is that he took care of his body and did not take care of his soul. When he speaks to himself, after he has made these big barns and filled them with goods, what word does he use to address himself? He speaks to his soul. He says, "Soul, you have it easy. Soul, we've taken care of you. Now you can take your ease, eat, drink and be merry." The mistake he made is that he had misunderstood the needs of his soul.

Our Lord comes and speaks to the man's soul. He says, "This night your soul will be required of you, and what good will these material possessions be to you then?" This man has spent his time caring for his material well-being, building up barns and taking care of his financial future, thinking that he was attending to the needs of his soul. But in the reality of death, it was clear that he had fed his soul the wrong food. He thought he was attending to his soul, he thought he had taken care of his needs—getting rid of the reason for anxiety, so that he could be peaceful and calm. Yet he had misunderstood, and he had not fed his soul.

There are many of us who are tempted to put the needs of our soul last. We think we will get around to the care of our soul after we have taken care of these other pressing needs. So there is a lesson for us in this parable about the importance of attending to our soul.

But there was a second mistake that this rich man made. Not only did he fail to feed his soul, but he also lived in the future. This is what he says to himself: "My soul, take it easy, because I have provided for many, many years." He lived for the future. The great irony is that there was no future for him on this earth, because our Lord says, "This night your soul will be required of you."

It is very tricky how Satan can tempt us to live in the future, to worry about our future, and to do everything so that our future is well taken care of. We forget about the needs of the present. I think this is what Jesus means when He says, "So is it for everyone who is rich toward himself and is not rich towards God." The rich man assumed that there would be time to take care of other things, and yet there was no time.

The great irony is that those who live for the future never get around to living for the present. You can take care of the next ten years, but then there's ten years after that. Once you embark on a life of preparing for the future, you never, ever get to the present, because there is always future. We can do this financially: we can think that the most important thing to do with our funds is to prepare for the future. How often have I heard, "I'll give to the poor after I've made sure that my future is taken care of." Your future is never taken care of, so you never give to the poor. There's always one more investment you need to make so that you're absolutely secure. And investments go up and down and the stock market is unpredictable.

This can happen financially; it can also happen intellectually. We can become so worried about what we're going to do. This is something that happens to young people. We become obsessed with, "What am I going to do in two years? What am I going to do in three years?" We become so future-oriented that we miss the opportunity to do good today.

You remember our Lord said in Matthew 6, "Don't worry about tomorrow. Tomorrow will take care of itself. Sufficient unto each day are the troubles thereof." Today is the day that has been given to us. Today is the day that God asks us to give our time and our money. Today is the day that God asks us not to lay up treasures for ourselves, but to be rich towards Him.

That's a very interesting line, isn't it? "So it will be with everyone who lays up treasure for himself and is not rich towards God." How can we be rich towards God? The amount of energy and time that we spend worrying about the future, we should devote to our relationship with God. We're rich towards God as we give to the ones that God loves—the poor and the needy. We're rich towards God as we spend time in prayer and in spiritual meditation.

We can waste a lot of time and a lot of money worrying and taking care of the future, and we can miss the opportunity that God has given us today. If we are rich towards God today, then God will take care of our future. He promised—and God doesn't break His promises. He said, "Seek first the kingdom of God and His righteousness, and all these things shall be added to you" (Matt. 6:33).

The great folly of planning for the future is that none of us knows what the future will hold. I heard about a woman who had planned for the future and invested in stock. The stock that she had crashed and she lost eighty percent of her retirement funds in a day. But if we invest in God today, then the one who knows the future will remember us. He will fulfill His promise.

There is a wonderful story in our tradition of a husband and wife who had a disagreement. They were poor and the husband was of the mindset that you have to take care and lay aside a little for emergencies. The wife was of the mindset that we should give away any extra we have to the poor. They had this ongoing debate, and finally the husband gave in and gave away the gold coins they had.

The wife said, "See, God will take care of us." In the next week or so, everything went wrong financially that could go wrong. You can imagine what that poor wife endured. Each day her husband said, "Yeah, God will take care of us, won't He?" They finally got to the point where they had nothing but a few coins. The husband berated his wife and said, "See—this is my last bit of money. I'm going to go out and buy our last meal. Then your God—what's He going to do for us?" He took that money, went out and bought a fish and some bread, and brought it home. When he opened up the fish, inside it was a bag with twice the number of gold coins he had given away in the beginning.

God will take care of us. If we are rich toward God, God will be rich to us. He will supply our needs and He will take care of our future. But if we become obsessed with worry and care for the future, if we become obsessed with our financial and material needs, then someday we will hear the words: "This night your soul will be required of you." And what good will all of your worries do you now? What good will all of your carefully planned financial arrangements be for you now, because this night you will stand before God. This night your soul will be required of you.

So let us use the time we have today wisely. Let us use it profitably. Let us be rich towards God. We are reminded of those words of Jesus for everyone who lays up treasure for himself: "Do not lay up for yourselves treasures on earth, where moth and rust destroy and where thieves break in and steal; but lay up for yourselves treasures in heaven, where neither moth nor rust destroys and where thieves do not break in and steal. For where your treasure is, there your heart will be also" (Matt. 6:19–21).

chapter 8

Putting Our Money Where Our Heart Is

Twenty-third Sunday after Pentecost
Luke 18:18–27

Now a certain ruler asked Him, saying, "Good Teacher, what shall I do to inherit eternal life?" So Jesus said to him, "Why do you call Me good? No one is good but One, that is, God. You know the commandments: 'Do not commit adultery,' 'Do not murder,' 'Do not steal,' 'Do not bear false witness,' 'Honor your father and your mother.'" And he said, "All these things I have kept from my youth." So when Jesus heard these things, He said to him, "You still lack one thing. Sell all that you have and distribute to the poor, and you will have treasure in heaven; and come, follow Me." But when he heard this, he became very sorrowful, for he was very rich.

And when Jesus saw that he became very sorrowful, He said, "How hard it is for those who have riches to enter the kingdom of God! For it is easier for a camel to go through the eye of a needle than for a rich man to enter the kingdom of God." And those who heard it said, "Who then can be saved?" But He said, "The things which are impossible with men are possible with God."

The Holy Church is a good mother, and good mothers know that you can't just tell people something once. A good mother knows that children don't pay attention. I remember the story of a young boy who was standing in a communion line when his family was visiting another church, and his mother wasn't standing next to him, because he had gone in front. As the mother was watching, a woman came over and said something to her young boy, very abruptly.

After the service, the mother asked her son, "What did that lady say to you?" And the boy said, "I don't know. I thought it was you, Mom, and I didn't pay any attention." Those of you who are mothers know that is true: children don't listen sometimes. Sometimes they have selective hearing. Sometimes, when it is the mother or the father speaking, they "tune them out."

The Holy Church is a good mother. She knows that sometimes we don't listen to what she says, so she says it over and over again. Two weeks ago our Gospel was the parable of the Good Samaritan; last week it was the parable of the rich fool. We were reminded again of the dangers of wealth and materialism, and of the necessity of giving to the poor. Today the Holy Church says, "In case you didn't get it two weeks ago, and in case you didn't get it last week, let me share one more story."

There was a man who came to Jesus and said, "Good Master, what must I do to inherit eternal life?" Jesus said, "Keep the commandments." The rich man said to Him, "I have kept them from my youth." Jesus said to him, "One thing you lack. Sell everything you have, give it to the poor, and you will have treasure in heaven."

In addition to the whole interchange between the rich young man and Jesus, we see something very significant in our Lord's words. He says, "Give to the poor, and you will have treasure in heaven." There are two other times in the Gospel of Luke where our Lord says a similar thing. "Sell what you have and give alms," He says, "provide yourselves money bags in heaven, which do not grow old" (Luke 12:33). "Give alms of such things as you have," He says, "then indeed all things are clean to you" (Luke 11:41).

Our Lord knows that the desire of our hearts is to be with Him in heaven and to enjoy paradise for eternity. He knows that we can become confused and wonder, "What is the way? What is the road that leads to paradise?" So He is very direct, very clear. He says, "Give to the poor, and you will have treasure in heaven." This is the message of the Advent Fast. If we are serious about desiring treasure in heaven, about wanting to spend eternity with the saints and with our Lord and His Holy Mother, then the way we prepare for heaven is through giving alms to the poor.

Of course, the rich young man who had come to Jesus didn't want to hear this message. He wanted Jesus to give him another road. He liked the road marked with, "Honor your father and your mother," because he could walk that road. He liked the road, "You shall not kill," because he had walked that road. "You shall not steal, you shall have no other gods before Me, you shall not bow down yourself to any graven image, you shall not bear false witness against your neighbor, remember the Sabbath day and keep it holy, you shall not take the name of the Lord your God in vain"—he had walked all those roads; they were fine with him.

But the road described by the tenth commandment, "You shall not covet," was a road that he had not walked. When the Lord quotes the commandments to this man, He does not quote the tenth commandment, because it was the tenth commandment that this man had broken again and again. If you have possessions, you can break the tenth commandment by coveting the possessions that you already have. If you do not have possessions, you can break it by coveting the possessions of others.

If we are to walk the road to heaven, we must face this tenth commandment. We must face the desires of our hearts. We must give alms to the poor, that we might have treasures in heaven. We talk about this over and over again. We read the writings of the Fathers. But reading the writings of the Fathers and hearing the words of the Gospel does not earn for us treasure in heaven. It's what our checkbook and bank accounts reveal that either earns for us treasure in heaven, or does not.

The simple question for us today is, "Have we listened to our Mother?" She's been very clear and straightforward. She has told us what we are to do. Are we like that young boy who immediately tuned out the words of his mother, or are we obedient children? What alms did you give this week? That's what you should be asking yourself today. What poor person did you feed? What naked person did you clothe? What sick person did you visit? What person who was without a house did you enable to have a dwelling place?

Jesus was not speaking words for His own benefit. We know

how the story ends. The rich young man hangs his face and leaves, because he was not willing to do what our Lord told him to do. He was willing to come to church. He was willing to kiss icons. He was willing to do metanoias and prostrations. He was willing to keep the fasts. He was willing to say long prayers. But he was not willing to give to the poor. And our Lord said to him, "None of the other stuff matters, if you are not willing to part with what you have and give it to those who have nothing."

Father Iakovos was a grace-bearing elder who died in 1991. Elder Iakovos grew up dirt poor. He was born in Asia Minor and was driven out by the Turks along with all the Greeks who were living there. He came to Greece, where the refugees had no land and worked as serfs for rich people. He grew up with absolutely nothing. Then he went to a monastery that had absolutely nothing. Yet Father Iakovos was known throughout the country as a great almsgiver, because he gave away everything. He gave away even what he didn't have. He considered it to be a waste of a day, if on that day he had not given something to someone.

There are wonderful stories told of his creativity and ingenuity in giving things away to the poor and needy. At the end of his life, God blessed him for all this giving. He had a moneybag. It was just a regular bag, in which he deposited anything anyone gave him— for prayers, or as a gift. Father Iakovos wouldn't even look at what was given, he'd just put it into this moneybag, which hung at the end of his bed. Whenever anyone would come and ask him for something, he would reach into this moneybag and whatever his hand grabbed, without counting it, he would give to the person who came. And that moneybag never grew empty. The more he gave away, the more God filled the bag. God honored His saint who gave to the poor.

I have a very dear friend who doesn't make a lot of money and has many financial obligations. From time to time, his bills stack up and they're more than he can pay. From time to time, he gets struck with that anxiety that all of us who live in the world have as he looks at these bills and looks at his checking account and knows that he's in way over his head again. This dear friend, whenever he feels that anxiety, always does the same thing: he goes to the bank and withdraws what he has left. Then he drives around until he finds a poor person and gives it all away.

I asked him once, "Why do you do that? Why do you give away, when you have very little and more bills than you know what to do with? Why, at that point, do you give it away?" And he said, "Because I have learned that God takes better care of paying my bills than I do. I have learned that the best investment I can make is the poor. And I can tell you that, over many years, God has met every single one of my needs. When I have had nothing and have still given, that is when God has opened the storehouses of heaven and rained His blessings on me."

We hear stories like those of Elder Iakovos and this friend of mine, but do we live these stories? Or do we think, "Isn't that wonderful!" but then make no change in the way we give? The words that we have heard will be our accusers on that great and final day. They will accuse us of unbelief because we don't believe that God can fill moneybags. They will accuse us of covetous hearts because we don't want to give away what we have. We will have to answer for whether we have heard our Holy Mother and obeyed her, or whether we have had hard hearts and closed our ears.

In the Old Testament, the Lord says to His people, "Circumcise your hearts" (cf. Deut. 10:16; Jer. 4:4). They had the externals, but their hearts were hard. The question for us this Advent is: what is the state of our hearts? There is nothing that reveals the state of your heart more clearly than your checkbook. If you brought your checkbook in and gave it to me, I could tell what you really care about. I could look and see how much money you spend on the poor, and how much money you spend on the Church, and how much money you spend on yourself. If the money you spend on yourself is greater than the money you spend on the poor and on God's Church, then I know where your heart is, because words are cheap.

That is what our Lord says to this rich young man: "Sell all that you have, and don't give me excuses. Sell all that you have and give it to the poor, and you will have treasure in heaven." And, of course, we say, "That's impossible. God didn't really mean that." But there was once a young man who was in church and heard this Gospel. That young man's name was Anthony. Anthony left the church, and as he walked out the door, he said, "You know, God said it and He meant it."

That week, he gave away everything he had and went out into the desert to live. That man became St. Anthony the Great, one of the greatest of the ascetics and one of the greatest of all the saints, because he was willing to listen to his Mother. He was willing to listen to his Lord and Master, and He was willing to do what he was told.

chapter 9

Lord, That I May See

Twenty-fourth Sunday after Pentecost
Luke 18:35–43

Then it happened, as He was coming near Jericho, that a certain blind man sat by the road begging. And hearing a multitude passing by, he asked what it meant. So they told him that Jesus of Nazareth was passing by. And he cried out, saying, "Jesus, Son of David, have mercy on me!" Then those who went before warned him that he should be quiet; but he cried out all the more, "Son of David, have mercy on me!" So Jesus stood still and commanded him to be brought to Him. And when he had come near, He asked him, saying, "What do you want Me to do for you?" He said, "Lord, that I may receive my sight." Then Jesus said to him, "Receive your sight; your faith has made you well." And immediately he received his sight, and followed Him, glorifying God. And all the people, when they saw it, gave praise to God.

In this Gospel we encounter a very familiar story: the blind man sitting by the side of the road. He is begging, as he is wont to do every day, sitting by the side of the road with nothing, being able to see nothing. This blind man hears the multitude, and asks what it means. He is told that Jesus of Nazareth is passing by. The blind man, as he has sat by the side of the road day after day, month after month, year after year, listening to life passing him by and being unable to enter into that life, in a moment of complete desperation sees that Jesus is his only hope. He sees that Jesus is the only possibility he has, and so from the depths of his soul comes that very singular cry: "Jesus, Son of David, have mercy on me!"

That is not a cry from the head. It is a cry from the depths of his being. The entire meaning of his life is wrapped up in this cry: "Jesus, Son of David, have mercy on me!" It is the cry of someone who has watched life pass him by. He wants so very much for life to come and visit him.

The crowds, who have been willing to tell him that Jesus is passing by, do not like this man crying to change the status quo. They tell him to be quiet. They say, "No, no. You are a beggar on the side of the road. That's your place. You be quiet and let us pass. Jesus has more important things to do than to listen to your cry."

How many times in his life has this blind man been told to be quiet? How many times has he listened? As he has begged for alms, those who have passed by have told him, "Be quiet, man. We don't want to hear it," and how many times has he allowed his voice to be silenced? How many times has he buried his head in his hands and shed tears, and not spoken and not believed?

But this time is different. This time it is Jesus who is passing by. He will not be silenced by the crowds. He will no longer accept his place as one who must sit and watch, or listen to, life passing him by. But he cries out incessantly: "Jesus, Son of David, have mercy on me!"

What is amazing for us is that with all the noise of a bustling crowd, with all the voices speaking on the road, our Lord Jesus hears the cry of this blind man, because our Lord's ears are attuned to cries of desperation, to cries that come from a heart of faith. Remember when our Lord was walking to see the daughter of Jairus, and many were touching Him in the crowds. Yet He felt the touch of the woman with an issue of blood. Just as He felt the touch of that woman, so He hears the cry of the blind man.

He stops the crowd. He stops the noise. He comes over and stands before this blind man, and says, "What is it that you want Me to do for you?" We see the kindness and gentleness of God. All his life, this blind man has had people telling him what he is to do. "Don't sit there. Don't beg so loud. You're not allowed to be here. Leave! This is not a place for you." God in the flesh does not come and tell him what to do, but, for the first time, He speaks to this blind man as one who has worth, as one who is made in the image of God, as one who deserves to be loved. He says, "What do you want Me to do for you?"

The blind man has been waiting all his life for that question. No one has ever asked the blind man, "What do you need? What do you want?" Out of his mouth comes that singular cry: "Lord, I want to see. Lord, I want my eyes to work. Lord, open my eyes." Our Lord looks at this blind man, whom the world has passed by, and He is moved by his faith and his need, and He says, "Be it unto you, according to your faith." The blind man is able to see.

What went through the heart of that blind man? St. Luke cannot put it into words, so he simply says, "And the blind man glorified God." What went through the heart of that blind man as he felt love, as he felt from God Himself the affirmation of his person, as he was given by God the ability to see? As the blind man opened his eyes and looked at the world, it looked very beautiful, this world that the crowds did not even notice: the beauty of the sky, the brilliance of the sun, the beauty in each human being's face, which is the beauty of God.

The crowds didn't even notice, but this blind man saw it. He saw because he had been given eyes by God Himself. Just as God in the flesh had seen the beauty of the blind man, so the blind man, given eyes by God, saw the beauty of the world. He saw the beauty of the Son of God. He saw the beauty of love.

This story, which is a very real story, is also a parable. It is told by Luke as a parable. We are the blind man, sitting by the road, and life and the world pass us by. We are in need of eyes. We also are the crowds who pass by the blind men of this world and tell them to be quiet, to recognize their place, and not to bother the Master. We are the crowds who, like the Pharisees, claim to see, but see only ourselves and thus do not see the beauty of God. The great tragedy of this parable is that every single human being on the road with Jesus needed to cry out, "Lord, that I may see." It wasn't only the blind man who needed new eyes; they all needed new eyes. Yet only the blind man asked, and only the blind man was given new eyes.

As we look at this parable and we look at our own lives, we are moved to be like the blind man, to cry out, "Lord Jesus Christ, Son of God, have mercy on me, a sinner!" When the Lord comes and says, "What is it that you want Me to do for you?" let us ask the Lord that we might be given new eyes, that we might be given eyes to see the beauty of creation, and in creation to see the beauty of God; that we might be given eyes to see the beauty of each human being, and in each human being to see the beauty of God; that we might be given eyes to see Jesus.

Jesus is coming. Soon we will celebrate the Nativity of the Son of God. That Nativity will be celebrated by millions around the world. How many will see only the gifts under the tree? How many will see only the eggnog, and the cookies, and the Christmas meal? How many of us will see Jesus? This parable is a reminder to us all that what we need to ask for most of all is new eyes, so that we might see, and in seeing, that we might glorify God, who has given such gifts to men.

chapter 10

Giving Birth to Christ in Our Hearts

Sunday of the Holy Ancestors of Christ
Matthew 1:1–25

> *The book of the genealogy of Jesus Christ, the Son of David, the Son of Abraham: Abraham begot Isaac, Isaac begot Jacob, and Jacob begot Judah and his brothers. Judah begot Perez and Zerah by Tamar, Perez begot Hezron, and Hezron begot Ram. Ram begot Amminadab, Amminadab begot Nahshon, and Nahshon begot Salmon. Salmon begot Boaz by Rahab, Boaz begot Obed by Ruth, Obed begot Jesse, and Jesse begot David the king. David the king begot Solomon by her who had been the wife of Uriah. Solomon begot Rehoboam, Rehoboam begot Abijah, and Abijah begot Asa. Asa begot Jehoshaphat, Jehoshaphat begot Joram, and Joram begot Uzziah. Uzziah begot Jotham, Jotham begot Ahaz, and Ahaz begot Hezekiah. Hezekiah begot Manasseh, Manasseh begot Amon, and Amon begot Josiah. Josiah begot Jeconiah and his brothers about the time they were carried away to Babylon. And after they were brought to Babylon, Jeconiah begot Shealtiel, and Shealtiel begot Zerubbabel. Zerubbabel begot Abiud, Abiud begot Eliakim, and Eliakim begot Azor. Azor begot Zadok, Zadok begot Achim, and Achim begot Eliud. Eliud begot Eleazar, Eleazar begot Matthan, and Matthan begot Jacob. And Jacob begot Joseph the husband of Mary, of whom was born Jesus who is called Christ. So all the generations from Abraham to David are fourteen generations, from David until the captivity in Babylon are fourteen generations, and from the captivity in Babylon until the Christ are fourteen generations.*
>
> *Now the birth of Jesus Christ was as follows: After His*

mother Mary was betrothed to Joseph, before they came together, she was found with child of the Holy Spirit. Then Joseph her husband, being a just man, and not wanting to make her a public example, was minded to put her away secretly. But while he thought about these things, behold, an angel of the Lord appeared to him in a dream, saying, "Joseph, son of David, do not be afraid to take to you Mary your wife, for that which is conceived in her is of the Holy Spirit. And she will bring forth a Son, and you shall call His name JESUS, for He will save His people from their sins." So all this was done that it might be fulfilled which was spoken by the Lord through the prophet, saying: "Behold, the virgin shall be with child, and bear a Son, and they shall call His name Immanuel," which is translated, "God with us." Then Joseph, being aroused from sleep, did as the angel of the Lord commanded him and took to him his wife, and did not know her till she had brought forth her first-born Son. And he called His name JESUS.

Today's Gospel is the genealogy of Christ. For those who know Old Testament history, there are a few names that stand out in the list. For example: "Judah begot Perez and Zerah by Tamar." Tamar was Judah's daughter-in-law. Her first two husbands, Judah's sons Er and Onan, died, and Judah refused to give her to his third son Shelah, as it was his duty to do. Then Tamar disguised herself as a harlot, deceived her father-in-law, and bore his child. It's a very unsightly passage. Yet Jesus comes from the line of Judah and Tamar.

A little later comes Rahab. Rahab was a harlot, a sinful woman, and she was not even an Israelite; she was a Canaanite. Our Lord has among his ancestors Rahab the harlot, the Gentile. Then a little later comes Ruth. Ruth was a virtuous woman, but she also was not an Israelite, but a Gentile.

Our Lord includes in His line an incestuous relationship (and the son born out of it) and a harlot. Then we find that of all the many sons of David, our Lord came from the line of Solomon, the son of Bathsheba. Bathsheba was the wife of Uriah, whom David had killed because Bathsheba was pregnant with David's child. It's very striking that in our Lord's line would be these prominent examples of sinfulness and depravity.

It is all the more striking when we think about His Mother, Mary, and her purity. We call her the Panagia, which means the All-holy One. The most pure Virgin Mary was chosen of God to be His Mother. We are told in our tradition that our Lord had to wait until there was a pure and holy one—He could not be born of just anyone, because the fire of His divinity would consume anyone who was filled with wickedness. Our Lord had to wait for this chosen Virgin, this holy, pure, and immaculate Virgin, who committed no actual sin, who was sheltered in the Temple and kept from the devices of the evil one and the temptations of the world. He could not be born of a sinful woman; He could only be born from a pure and holy Mother.

On the one hand we have the paragon of virtue, the height of innocence and virginity, and at the same time we have wickedness and depravity in His ancestry. What is it that the Gospel writer wants to teach us by this juxtaposition of holy and sinful people in the line of our Lord God and Savior Jesus Christ?

There are two lessons presented here. The first is that our Lord came to save those who are sinners. The wonderful announcement that is found right in the beginning of St. Matthew's Gospel is that our Lord did not come only for the righteous. In fact, He Himself said over and over again, "I have not come to call the righteous, but sinners to repentance." Over and over again He said, "I am not come for the healthy, but that I might bring healing to those who are sick, and those who are struggling and suffering with the illness of sin and depravity" (cf. Matt. 9:13; Mark 2:17; Luke 5:32).

So we are reminded by His genealogy that the sins of our past do not keep God from saving us. No matter what we have done, God's love is greater than our sin. The Apostle Paul wrote, "Where sin abounded, grace abounded much more" (Romans 5:20). Our Lord came not to dwell with the righteous, or the rich, or those who were acceptable in society. As the Pharisees said with horror: "He lives with publicans and sinners, He is a friend of harlots and tax collectors" (cf. Luke 5:30; 7:34).

Our Lord came to save those who were lost in sin, to heal those who were made sick by sin. Whatever sin we may carry in our past is not greater than the love of God. It does not keep God from accepting us and using us. Think about it: a harlot, one who had lived in sin, became an ancestress of God in the flesh. There is no sin that is greater than the love of God.

This Christmas as we celebrate the Incarnation of Christ, we are made joyful by the reality that He came to live with people like you and me. All of us have skeletons in our closets. We hide those things, and then we mention them in confession and hang our heads. We are so thankful that the priest is under an obligation never to share those things with anyone, because it would be awful, we think, if others knew.

Yet this Christmas we are reminded that God knows everything, and yet God does not recoil from us. God does not step back from us and say, "Oh, such awful people!" In knowing everything, God reaches out His arms to us and embraces us with His love. St. Paul's Letter to the Hebrews says that God is not ashamed to call us His brothers and sisters (Heb. 2:11). He's not ashamed to count us who have committed great sins as belonging to Him. He does not reject us, but accepts us, reaches out to us, and embraces us in His love.

So we are reminded first, as we come to celebrate this Feast of the Nativity, that there is no sin that is greater than God's love, and that God longs to gather us all. God will never push us away. But as we stop and think not only about the genealogy, which is filled with these terrible sinners, but also about the most pure Virgin, we are reminded of another truth. While God loves all of us in our sin and does not reject us because of our sin, we have to choose between sin and God. We cannot cling to sin in our hearts and expect the Lord Jesus to make His home in our hearts at the same time.

All the sinners found in this genealogy are characterized not only by their sin. They are also characterized by their repentance. Rahab, it is true, was a harlot. But she showed great faith in accepting the Israelite spies, and she risked her life to save the spies who had been sent. Her faith and her repentance brought her into the family of God.

Ruth grew up as a pagan. But she said to Naomi, her mother-in-law, "Your people *shall be* my people, and your God, my God. Where you die, I will die, and there will I be buried" (Ruth 1:16, 17). Unlike the other daughter-in-law of Naomi, who turned and went back to Moab, Ruth turned her back on Moab and her pagan life. In repentance she journeyed to the land of Israel, and she lived a repentant and holy life.

Consider David and Bathsheba. Yes, there was great sin—adultery and murder. But there was also great repentance. David, we know, penned Psalm 50: "Have mercy on me, O God, according to Your great goodness. According to the multitude of Your tender compassions blot out my iniquities, for I acknowledge my transgressions and my sin is ever before me. Against You and You only have I sinned and done that which is evil in Your sight."

So this Nativity, as we prepare to celebrate the birth of our great God and Savior Jesus Christ, we must realize that in order for Christ to make His home in our hearts, it is necessary for us to turn our backs on sin. Our sin cannot keep God from us, unless we hold onto our sin and cherish it. St. John says: "If we say that we have no sin, we deceive ourselves, and the truth is not in us." But he goes on to say that if we confess our sins, God is faithful and just to forgive us our sins, and to cleanse us from all unrighteousness (1 John 1:8, 9).

All of us have sinned; we will never be like the Mother of God, pure and immaculate and without stain. But we can be like the harlot who recognized her sin and hated it, who came to Jesus and fell at His feet, washed His feet with her tears, and dried them with her hair. As we come to celebrate the Feast of Our Lord's Nativity, let us bring to the Lord our repentance. Let us make a clean break with sin. Let us turn our backs on anything that would drive Christ from us, and in humility and repentance let us invite Christ to come and be born in our hearts.

The ancient tradition was to put a candle in your window on the Eve of Nativity. In the ancient world, if there was room for travelers, you put a candle in the window. If there was no room for travelers, you blew the candle out. There was no Motel 6 or Super 8 in those days—travelers stayed in people's homes. So as you were traveling and you came into a town, you would look for a candle in the window, and you would know that you could go to that home and find lodging. The Christians throughout the ages, on the Eve of the Feast of Nativity, would put candles in their windows, as a sign that their homes and their hearts were open to the Christ Child, and that they desired Him to be born within on that Christmas morn.

Beloved, let us put candles in the windows of our hearts. Let us clean our hearts and drive out all the dirtiness and uncleanness of sin, so that when Jesus comes, He will be born in us anew. That's the wonderful thing about the Feast of Nativity—it's fresh and new every year.

Like the Mother of God, we cherish these things in our hearts. Each Nativity we cherish the newborn Christ, and we ask Him to be born within us. We ask Him to complete the work of repentance in us, because we cannot wholly repent. We try, but we can't. We scrub and we scrub, and when we get done there's still sin sticking to the walls. This Christmas we ask that Christ would come and finish the work which we have begun, that He would cleanse our hearts of all impurity, and that He would do the impossible—that He would take sinners like you and me and make us as pure as His Holy Mother.

St. Simeon the New Theologian says that we should not think that the Mother of God is the only one who can give birth to Christ. He says in a mystical way, each Christian is called to be a Theotokos, a God-bearer. Each Christian is called to receive God and to give birth to God in this world.

chapter 11

Joseph the Protector

Sunday after the Nativity
Matthew 2:13–23

Now when they had departed, behold, an angel of the Lord appeared to Joseph in a dream, saying, "Arise, take the young Child and His mother, flee to Egypt, and stay there until I bring you word; for Herod will seek the young Child to destroy Him." When he arose, he took the young Child and His mother by night and departed for Egypt, and was there until the death of Herod, that it might be fulfilled which was spoken by the Lord through the prophet, saying, "Out of Egypt I called My Son."

Then Herod, when he saw that he was deceived by the wise men, was exceedingly angry; and he sent forth and put to death all the male children who were in Bethlehem and in all its districts, from two years old and under, according to the time which he had determined from the wise men. Then was fulfilled what was spoken by Jeremiah the prophet, saying:

"A voice was heard in Ramah,
Lamentation, weeping, and great mourning,
Rachel weeping for her children,
Refusing to be comforted,
Because they are no more."

But when Herod was dead, behold, an angel of the Lord appeared in a dream to Joseph in Egypt, saying, "Arise, take the young Child and His mother, and go to the land of Israel, for those who sought the young Child's life are dead." Then he arose, took the young Child and His mother, and came into the land of Israel. But when he heard that Archelaus was reigning over

Judea instead of his father Herod, he was afraid to go there. And being warned by God in a dream, he turned aside into the region of Galilee. And he came and dwelt in a city called Nazareth, that it might be fulfilled which was spoken by the prophets, "He shall be called a Nazarene."

On this Sunday we commemorate those men who were so significant in the life of our Lord. Even though there was no man who was His father, at the same time we recognize that there were significant men who attended to Christ and watched over Him. Just as Mary undid the trespass of Eve, so these holy and righteous men undid the trespass of Adam.

In the Garden, the failure of Eve was disobedience. She did not say to the Lord, "Be it unto me according to Your word," but rather she reached out and said, "Be it unto me according to my desire." So Mary, who is the second Eve, undoes the trespass of the first Eve by rejecting her own desires and acting not in accordance with the lust of the eyes or the lust of the flesh, but in accordance with the will of God.

Now what is the trespass of Adam in the Garden? Adam's sin was that he did not watch over and protect his wife from the evil one. Eve went to Adam and gave him the fruit. Instead of protecting her from sin and standing between her and the evil one, Adam followed the lead of Eve and partook of the food with her. Adam had been placed in the Garden to watch over and protect his wife from evil, but he failed.

Joseph avoids the trespass of Adam. We call Joseph two things: the Betrothed (because we recognize that he was not married to the Virgin Mary as we are married to our spouses), and also the Protector, because he watched over this woman who had been given to him by God. He protected her from the wiles of the evil one.

In the Orthodox celebration of the Nativity, it is the Gospel of Matthew upon which we meditate. (In the West, it's the Gospel of St. Luke.) We read Matthew 2:13–23 on the day after Christmas and again on the celebration of the Holy Innocents, and on the Sunday after Nativity we read it again. Why does the Church love that passage so much? Why is that passage so critical in our celebration of the Nativity?

It parallels what took place in the Garden. In the Garden, Satan did not come as himself, but used the serpent to deceive Eve and Adam. When Jesus is born, Satan uses another serpent, only this serpent is Herod. Just as the serpent tried to deceive Eve, so Herod tries to deceive the Magi: "Come back and tell me where He is, so that I might come and worship Him." Satan works through Herod and attempts to deceive, so that he might destroy the salvation of mankind.

Joseph, the Protector, stands in the bridge. Joseph the Protector does not allow the deception to occur. Being warned by God in a dream, he acts to protect the Virgin Mary and this little Child from the machinations of the evil one. Today we honor him for his role as protector. We honor him because he was willing to listen to the voice of the angel.

Joseph is guided through dreams. He has a dream and recognizes that this Child is indeed the Son of God. He has another dream and goes down to Egypt to protect the Son of God and His Virgin Mother. Then he is warned of God in a dream again that it is time to return. He returns not to Judea, but to Nazareth, because he knows (through another dream) that the son of the evil serpent is on the throne and that the son is as bad as the father. (That son of Herod is the one who condemned St. John the Baptist and took off his head.) So we give honor to Joseph today as the Protector.

We also honor James, the brother of the Lord. Icons of the Descent into Egypt show Mary and the Baby and Joseph, and a young man who is leading the donkey. That young man is James, the brother (technically, the stepbrother) of the Lord, who was faithful, who recognized Christ and joined together with his own father Joseph to form a protective cover for the Virgin Mary and the Incarnate Christ.

Today we give honor to these men who understood what is really the essence of masculinity. If the Virgin Mary is the icon of what it means to be a woman, in that she received Christ and "kept all these things and pondered them in her heart" (Luke 2:19; cf.

also Luke 2:51), so with Joseph and James we see the icon of what it means to be male, what it means to be a father and a husband. To be male is to protect the innocent, those who are vulnerable and can be abused, to spread our wings of protection and care over those who have been entrusted to us, to keep them from the machinations and wiles of the evil one.

There is something else that is very striking as we come to the end of our celebration of the Nativity. Where do the Magi come from? They come from Babylon. Where does Jesus go, when He is an infant? He goes to Egypt. If you go through the Old Testament carefully, you will find that according to the Old Testament the cesspools of iniquity, the places from which evil always arises, are Babylon and Egypt. We even see it in the Book of Revelation with the Whore of Babylon. Egypt is a place of iniquity and abuse and sin. And yet in our Lord's birth the people from Babylon come to worship Him, and He goes to Egypt to sanctify that land.

Our Lord has come to save the world. Our Lord was born to bring the nations under one leader, "even God Himself." We see the message of our salvation, because we are the Babylonians and we are the Egyptians. We are the Gentiles, and our Lord has come to bring salvation to us.

St. Mark begins his Gospel by saying, "The beginning of the Gospel of Jesus Christ," and then he immediately goes on to speak of the man who appeared in the wilderness by the name of John the Baptist. He was the voice of one crying in the wilderness, "Prepare the way of the Lord." We can see how our celebration of the Nativity leads us to Theophany, to our celebration of the Lord's Baptism and the revelation of the Holy Trinity. The connection between Christmas and Theophany is found in the person and message of St. John: "Prepare the way of the Lord."

Our Lord has been born to bring salvation to the Babylonians and the Egyptians, to sinners like you and me. But He cannot save us if we do not work together with Him, if we do not prepare the way of the Lord. St. John proclaimed, "Repent, for the kingdom of heaven is at hand!" (Matt. 3:2). We cannot save ourselves—that's why Jesus came. But Jesus cannot save us unless we repent.

Very soon, we will hear this word: "Let us turn our eyes from Bethlehem and look to the Jordan." Let us turn our eyes from the Babe born in the manger to the Son of God being baptized in the waters. Let us walk with Him as He leaves Egypt and goes to the place of dedication, because He will be called the Nazarene, and the word Nazarene in Hebrew means "dedicated." He will be called a consecrated one.

Let us follow Him from the Egypt of our passions and desires and sin. Let us leave the Babylon of our lusts, and let us go to the place of consecration and dedication. Let us make straight the ways and paths of the Lord and let us go to the waters of the Jordan, that we might be united to Christ in His death and be raised to the newness of life.

chapter 12

The Joy of Confession

Sunday before Theophany

Mark 1:1–8

*The beginning of the gospel of Jesus Christ, the Son of God.
As it is written in the Prophets:*

> *"Behold, I send My messenger before Your face,
> Who will prepare Your way before You.
> The voice of one crying in the wilderness:
> 'Prepare the way of the LORD;
> Make His paths straight.'"*

John came baptizing in the wilderness and preaching a baptism of repentance for the remission of sins. Then all the land of Judea, and those from Jerusalem, went out to him and were all baptized by him in the Jordan River, confessing their sins. Now John was clothed with camel's hair and with a leather belt around his waist, and he ate locusts and wild honey. And he preached, saying, "There comes One after me who is mightier than I, whose sandal strap I am not worthy to stoop down and loose. I indeed baptized you with water, but He will baptize you with the Holy Spirit."

The feast of the Theophany is very rich and very deep; there is much for us to learn and ponder and much grace to be poured out upon us. On this Sunday before Theophany, the Holy Church puts before us the image of John the Baptist, thus reminding us that before grace is poured out upon us, we must prepare ourselves to receive it. When we plant a garden, it is necessary for us to break the ground, plow, fertilize, and weed it, so that we can plant the seed and water it, so then it can sprout. In the same way it is necessary for us to prepare our hearts.

John came preaching a baptism of repentance. What is necessary for us in order that we may receive the grace of God? What is necessary, first and foremost, is that we be honest about our sins. We prefer to cover our sin. We like to hide it from ourselves and especially from others, to keep all the depravity and wickedness of our souls under wraps, and then to present to everyone we see a persona of holiness and correctness.

We cannot be cured if we hide our sins, or make excuses for our sins, or pretend that we have no sins. We can only be healed when we confess our sin: when we confess, first of all to ourselves, then to others, that we struggle, we are sinful, we are proud, we are arrogant, we are angry, we are jealous, we are covetous; and most importantly, when we confess it to God. We can only be healed if we are honest about our sins.

Sometimes we hide from our sins because we are afraid. We are afraid that if we admit our struggles we will be admitting our powerlessness; we are afraid that somehow the admission of our sin will mean that we are forever doomed by our sin. If we admit the wickedness that is within us, then we will have to admit that we can't change ourselves.

Hear the word of John, and indeed the word of God: if we are honest about our sin, then it will not enslave us. Honesty and confession will set us free. It's a lie of Satan that keeps us afraid of sin— so afraid that we don't want to look into our souls. Sin's power over us, and Satan's entrapment of us, can only operate in the dark. When we hide, when we are not honest, then sin is powerful and Satan can do his deeds.

When we are honest about our sin, sin loses its grip. When we allow the light of confession to shine into our souls, Satan can no longer work there. That's why some monastics practice the confession of thoughts. In monasteries where there is a holy elder, every monastic goes before the elder or eldress each night and confesses all of his or her thoughts, not just the sinful ones: they confess every single thought that they can remember, because there is freedom in confession. There is freedom from sin and from the snares of the evil one when we confess our sins, when we verbalize the struggles within our soul.

But what happens if we don't confess our sins? We get lost in what I call the labyrinth of our own thinking. When we isolate ourselves and do not confess our sins, then Satan is very good at confusing us. We can get lost in the intricacies of our own thinking.

John came preaching a baptism of repentance. If we look throughout history, the great movements of the Spirit of God always follow after great times of confession. My own patron, St. John of Kronstadt, was a wonderworking priest in the city of Kronstadt in Russia at the turn of the century. The grace that was within him called forth the confession of the people of God. Before services began there would be six or seven thousand people in the cathedral. He would come out and pray over them, and they would all pour forth their confessions.

We struggle with confessing our sins to the priest even when the doors are shut and we can whisper. In the days of St. John, thousands confessed their sins together. They screamed at the top of their lungs, they wept, they fell on the floor confessing their sins, baring their souls for the world to see. Those who confessed were healed. In order for the grace of God to operate in our souls, we must abandon pride, we must put away our fear, and we must be honest: honest with ourselves; honest with each other, because we are a family and we know that we are all sinners; and most importantly, honest with God.

We confess to God our struggles, our disappointments, our anger, our jealousy. In the Vespers service we are instructed to pour out our hearts to God, to be open before God with no pretense, hypocrisy, justification, or fear. Our God is a loving God who wants to heal us. He is not a God who will reject us if we are open with Him. The great irony is that we close up because we fear God's rejection, but it is the very fact that we have closed up that makes us feel God's rejection. "The one who comes to Me," said Jesus, "I will by no means cast out" (John 6:37).

God has never turned away anyone because he has confessed

his sin. God has never said to anyone who confessed, "Enough! I don't want to see you. I can't take your sin anymore." (He did say that to hypocrites who pretended they had no sin; see, for example, Isaiah 43:22–24.) God said, "Come to Me, all you who labor and are heavy laden, and I will give you rest" (Matt. 11:28).

Come unto Me, open yourself before Me. Be real. Come to the Jordan confessing your sins, and My Spirit will descend upon this water. And in descending upon this water, My Spirit will descend upon you, and you will be cleansed, you will be healed, and you will be set free. Confession, repentance, honesty: this is what we must do, so that God can pour out His grace upon us, so that we might be delivered, so that we might be saved.

chapter 13

The Necessity of Repentance

Sunday after Theophany
Matthew 4:12–17
Now when Jesus heard that John had been put in prison, He departed to Galilee. And leaving Nazareth, He came and dwelt in Capernaum, which is by the sea, in the regions of Zebulun and Naphtali, that it might be fulfilled which was spoken by Isaiah the prophet, saying:

> *"The land of Zebulun and the land of Naphtali,*
> *By the way of the sea, beyond the Jordan,*
> *Galilee of the Gentiles:*
> *The people who sat in darkness have seen a great light,*
> *And upon those who sat in the region and shadow of death*
> *Light has dawned."*

From that time Jesus began to preach and to say, "Repent, for the kingdom of heaven is at hand."

It is striking to me that the first words that come out of our Lord's mouth as He begins His ministry after His Baptism are: "Repent, for the kingdom of heaven is at hand." Those words are the very same words that John the Baptist spoke at the advent of his ministry. John came preaching a baptism of repentance, and the crowds flocked to him from Jerusalem, Judea, Galilee, and Samaria. John said to them the very same words that Jesus said: "Repent, for the kingdom of heaven is at hand" (Matt. 3:2).

The word *repent* has deep meaning. But at its most basic, the word *repent* is a clarion call to change. It is striking that Jesus—as He is publicly revealed, as He has been shown to be the Son of God at His Baptism—comes forth and begins His ministry by saying, "You must change, the kingdom of heaven is at hand."

Our Lord's message demands of us change. Throughout the Gospels Jesus makes it very clear that those who will follow Him are going to have to change the way they live; He will not let them follow Him and remain as they were. He is very clear that He is God, and as God He intends to make demands on His followers. They cannot follow Him and merely add Him to their life as it already is; in following Him the very structure and fabric of their life will be challenged and changed.

We see this in many ways in the Gospel. The multitudes came to Jesus and He said, "Follow Me." They said, "Where do You live?" He said, "Foxes have holes and birds of the air have their nests, but the Son of Man has nowhere to lay His head. Follow Me." One said to Him, "First I will bury my dead and then I will follow You," and Jesus said, "That doesn't cut it. Let the dead bury the dead, but you follow Me. I have come to radically restructure your life, I have come to change."

Others said to Him, "Lord, we will follow You, but let us finish our business engagements." Jesus said, "That doesn't cut it. Whoever puts his hand to the plow and looks back is not worthy of being My disciple" (cf. Matt. 8:19–22; Luke 9:57–62).

Repent, for the kingdom of heaven is at hand. Jesus comes to us today, after we have celebrated His Baptism. He stands before us today and says the very same thing John said: "Repent, for the kingdom of heaven is at hand. I have come not to make your life comfortable. I have come to radically restructure your life. I have come to make demands on you. I have come to change you. Repent, for the kingdom of heaven is at hand."

The great tragedy of being a Christian in the twenty-first century—indeed, the great tragedy of following Christ throughout the years—is that we can begin with great enthusiasm. When my family originally came into Orthodoxy, there was nothing that we would not do for Christ. It was a joy for us to fast, it was a joy for us to come to church, and in the beginning we were at every service: vespers, orthros, early morning liturgies throughout the week. We read every book we could get our hands on. We prayed, we cut all our entanglements with the world, and we pursued God with great enthusiasm, because we were aware of the fact that we had found the pearl of great price.

But something happens. It's hard to follow Christ with commitment. It's easy for us to lose that enthusiasm and to fall back into the patterns of our old life. It's easy for us to be tired and to skip our prayers. It's easy for us to look at the clock on Sunday morning, when it rings early enough for us to come to orthros, and say that we're tired and we've had a long week. We'll hit the snooze button once, or twice, or three times. We'll be there for liturgy, because what is one orthros?

It's easy for us on Saturday evenings, because we're tired and we've been driving, to say, "Let's stay home tonight." It's easy for us to fall back into the habit of allowing our Saturday evenings to become times when we watch television and entertain ourselves, instead of times, as the Holy Church prescribes, of prayer and quiet and meditation and preparation for Holy Communion.

Our Lord comes this morning and stands before us in His glory. He says, "Repent." You remember that our Lord comes to the church of Ephesus in the Book of Revelation (2:4, 5) and says, "You have lost your first love. Remember therefore from where you have fallen. Remember the zeal that you once had, remember the enthusiasm you once had, and repent, change, for the kingdom of heaven is at hand."

Our Lord will not allow us to become complacent. He will not allow us to make Him a *part* of our lives. He demands one hundred percent commitment from us. He demands that He *be* our life. He demands of us that we be willing to let go of anything that takes us from Him. "Repent, for the kingdom of heaven is at hand."

We need to love God more than anything or anyone. The love of God must consume our souls, so that we can say with the psalmist, "Whom have I in heaven *but You?* / And *there is* none upon earth *that* I desire besides You. / My flesh and my heart fail; / But God is the strength of my heart and my portion forever" (Ps. 73:25, 26).

Our hearts need to be on fire for God, to love Him with a

passion that is so strong that all other loves seem to us to be hatred. Jesus said, "If anyone comes to Me and does not hate his father and mother, wife and children, brothers and sisters, yes, and his own life also, he cannot be My disciple" (Luke 14:26). Our love for God is to be so strong that in comparison everything else seems to be hatred.

God comes to us today and says, "Repent. You have allowed other loves to creep into your heart. You have allowed yourself to be distracted and to forget what is important. You have allowed the mantra of this world, which says, 'Do not be a fanatic, do not be too zealous for your faith,' to take you away from your zeal for God." God comes at this time of renewal, and He says to us, "Repent, for the kingdom of heaven is at hand."

Someday soon, all of this will be gone. This world will be consumed by fire, and all that we have lived for and worked for will be destroyed. The only thing that will remain is our heart. The only thing that will endure that fire is God, and what we have done for God. Repent, for the kingdom of heaven is at hand. Change now, before it is too late. Change now, before our Lord returns. Change now, for the kingdom of heaven is at hand.

chapter 14

Living Forgiven and Thankful Lives, Part One

Thirty-third Sunday After Pentecost
Luke 17:12–19

Then as He entered a certain village, there met Him ten men who were lepers, who stood afar off. And they lifted up their voices and said, "Jesus, Master, have mercy on us!" So when He saw them, He said to them, "Go, show yourselves to the priests." And so it was that as they went, they were cleansed. And one of them, when he saw that he was healed, returned, and with a loud voice glorified God, and fell down on his face at His feet, giving Him thanks. And he was a Samaritan. So Jesus answered and said, "Were there not ten cleansed? But where are the nine? Were there not any found who returned to give glory to God except this foreigner?" And He said to him, "Arise, go your way. Your faith has made you well."

We learn a great deal about the spiritual life and what it means to follow Christ, not only from our successes. It can be said that we learn even more from our failures and mistakes. This is what I have learned in my own spiritual life: there are things that are revealed to us when we fail that we can only learn through failure.

One of the greatest tools of Satan is to get us so focused on our need, on what we are lacking, that we fall into despair. We become so aware of our sin and our passions, so aware of what we lack, that the awareness itself is crushing to our spirits, and we fall into despair and do not find healing.

This Gospel is about ten lepers who had the faith in the midst of their need to cry out, "Jesus, Son of David, have mercy on us."

Perhaps there were other lepers there who were so aware of their need that they had despaired of ever being healed. So they did not bother to pray.

But on the other side there is another danger. (If Satan can't get us from one side, he'll attack us from the other!) If the first great danger is to focus on our need and come to despair, the second great danger is to focus on our health and forget that we were ever in need. This is what happened to nine of our ten lepers. In their great need all ten cried out, "Jesus, Son of David, have mercy on us." And all ten were healed. Jesus simply said, "Go to the priests," and as they went they were healed.

Then the nine looked at their healed bodies and became so filled with joy and wonder and amazement that their fingers worked, they could feel their hands, and their flesh was not white anymore that they forgot that just a few minutes earlier, they had been lepers. In their eagerness to go home, they ran to the priests and received their blessing. They went home and embraced their families and rejoiced in their health—and forgot the One who had healed them.

There was only one man who looked at his flesh and said, "My flesh, which just a few minutes ago was leprous, is now beautiful. Just a few minutes ago, I could not approach a human being, but had to stand and cry, 'Unclean, unclean!' But now I can embrace my loved ones, now I can hug my wife and children. How did I become healed? How did this happen to me? All I know is that a minute ago I was a leper, and now I am clean." He, aware both of his health and of his sickness, went running to Jesus, fell on his knees and proclaimed his thanksgiving.

He remembered his need, and he remembered the One who healed him. He knew that just as he had been healed in a moment, so too he could become leprous again in a moment. He fell down and cried, "Jesus, Son of David, have mercy."

There is a story in our tradition of a very holy elder who in his youth had struggled with lust and who had, through his struggle and through the grace of God, been healed of his spiritual illness. The Synaxarion says that he was grace-filled and became clairvoyant; in fact, it says that he was perfect. He was completely healed.

He then was given the charge by the Mother of God to receive visitors and give spiritual counsel, because he had been healed so that he in turn could heal others.

Many came to him from the cities. One day a young woman came to him wanting spiritual counsel. As the story is told, the elder became so filled with lust for her that he abused her terribly. After he had abused her, he was so remorseful that he murdered her so that she would never tell anyone what he had done. Then he was so afraid of what he had done that he buried her body out in the desert and told no one. Only then did he wake up and realize what he had done.

We read that story and say, "How can a clairvoyant elder, who is able to read the souls of those who come to him, who is perfect and speaks personally to God, fall into such terrible sin?" The Synaxarion tells us: because he forgot that he had once been sick. Because he forgot that it was God who had healed him, he forgot that his only hope was in the grace of God, and if God removed that grace even for an instant, he would be as sick as he had been when he began the struggle.

At Alcoholics Anonymous, alcoholics are taught that the most important thing they have to remember in order to be healed is that they are always alcoholics. If you talk to someone who has struggled through alcoholism and is now clean and sober, he will tell you that he is only one drink away from falling back into drunkenness. One drink away! And if he ever forgets that he is an alcoholic who is one drink away from drunkenness, then he will fall back into the sickness from which he has been cleansed.

How often do we forget that this is also true of us: it is not our labors that have done anything. It is God's grace. And all those sins we committed in the past, which by God's grace we no longer commit, we could commit today, if for an instant God's grace were withdrawn from us. We are only clean—to whatever extent we are clean—because of the grace of God.

If you ever have the blessing of speaking to a holy elder or eldress, you know that he or she is very holy and there's no sin in them. Yet you will find that they say such things as, "What are you coming to me for? I'm just like you, I'm just flesh and blood, a sinner. I'm weak and I'm nothing." And you look at them and say, "What do you mean, you're just like me? Thank God you're not just like me, that's why I'm coming to you, because you're different from me, and you're not just flesh and blood! You're holy, and when you walk the light of God shines from you!"

They look back at you and say, "No, you must have me confused with the man who lives next door, because I'm just like you." We wonder, how can they say this? How could the saints who don't sin say, "I'm weak"? We think that it must be false humility, that they are accusing themselves of things that they didn't do wrong.

But in fact, the saints are so humble because they always bear the consciousness that once they were sick, and that it was God who made them whole. They bear in their souls the understanding that if God should withdraw His grace for a second, they would fall back into those very same sins from which they came.

St. Macarios the Great used to sit outside his cell in the Egyptian desert and weep all day. Even when he was an old man, and he was too old and tired to do anything wrong, he would weep because of his sin. His disciples would come up to him and say, "Father, what are you weeping about? We've watched you all day and you haven't even moved. How could you do anything bad enough to weep about, when you don't even move?"

He would weep and say, "When I was eight years old, there were boys who went into my next-door neighbor's orchard and stole apples. They ran with their bags full of apples and one of the apples fell out in front of me, and I picked it up and ate it." Then he would start to weep profusely. "I am such an awful sinner!"

We read that, and we think, "What, you were eight years old, and now you're eighty, and you're still weeping about an apple? Tell me the name of your neighbor and I'll go pay for the apple, just so that you can stop weeping."

But he wasn't weeping because he thought he had not been forgiven for that sin. He was weeping because he knew that he was still that weak child. He could be sitting there, and sin could roll in front of him, and without thinking he could reach out and take that sin and eat it. He knew that no matter how high he was, in an instant he could fall. So every day he mourned, and yet every day he was filled with great joy because he gave thanks to God. Although he was weak, he knew that God's grace had preserved him.

John 9 tells the story of the man blind from birth, whom Jesus healed and who was then hauled into court. The Pharisees had a long list of questions: "Who healed you and by what power did he heal you? Why did he heal you and how? What's the meaning of this healing, what's the agenda behind it? What's going on here?" The blind man simply said, "I don't know, I only know one thing. Once I was blind; now I can see."

May God give us the grace to see that we will always be recovering sinners, never healed, but always in the process of being healed. No matter how high we go, no matter how much God's grace visits us, no matter how many experiences of God we have, may we always say, "I don't know how or why, I only know that once I was blind, but now I can see."

chapter 15

Living Forgiven and Thankful Lives, Part Two

Thirty-fourth Sunday after Pentecost
Luke 18:35–43

Then it happened, as He was coming near Jericho, that a certain blind man sat by the road begging. And hearing a multitude passing by, he asked what it meant. So they told him that Jesus of Nazareth was passing by. And he cried out, saying, "Jesus, Son of David, have mercy on me!" Then those who went before warned him that he should be quiet; but he cried out all the more, "Son of David, have mercy on me!" So Jesus stood still and commanded him to be brought to Him. And when he had come near, He asked him, saying, "What do you want Me to do for you?" He said, "Lord, that I may receive my sight." Then Jesus said to him, "Receive your sight; your faith has made you well." And immediately he received his sight, and followed Him, glorifying God. And all the people, when they saw it, gave praise to God.

The message of this Gospel reading is ultimately one that commends to us perseverance. The blind man continued to cry out, even though all those around him tried to silence him. The blind man's cry, "Jesus, Son of David, have mercy on me," is the most natural cry of a human soul. Any other cry is unnatural. You would think, if it is natural to us, that it would be easy for us to say, "Jesus, Son of God, have mercy on me, a sinner," and you would think that everyone around us would encourage us in this prayer, because it is the most important prayer that any of us can utter.

But those of you who have prayed know that what should be

easy is not easy at all. You know that what should be the most natural response of our hearts is something for which we have to struggle. There are many voices that tell us to be quiet. Sometimes this is the voice of our pride: "Why do you cry out all the time, have mercy on me? You don't need to pray that prayer any more; you are beyond that."

Sometimes it is the voice of distraction, which says, "There are more interesting things to do. There are things which will be more important for you. There are things that you can be involved in that will give you more fun."

Sometimes the voices are the voices of sin, the voice of lust, the voice of anger, both of which enter into our soul and corrupt it so that we can no longer pray in clarity, "Jesus, Son of God, have mercy on me, a sinner." The voice of self-love also seeks to silence our prayer.

Sometimes the voices that seek to silence us are the voices of our friends and families, who call us to leave behind the work of prayer so that we might devote ourselves to the things they are interested in and the things they want us to do. Then there is the voice of despair that says you are beyond the mercy of God.

Sometimes—and perhaps this is the most difficult one of all— the voice that seeks to silence us is the voice of silence itself. How often have you prayed, "Jesus, Son of God, have mercy on me, a sinner," and experienced in response not the voice of God, but rather the voice of silence. You feel as if there is no response to your prayer. You feel as if the heavens are shut up and your prayer does not even ascend to the throne of God.

All of these voices seek to silence our prayer. In the words of the Gospel, they seek to persuade us to hold our peace, to be quiet, and to let Jesus pass by.

Prayer is a struggle, and the struggle of prayer is not simply the struggle to make time for prayer. The struggle to get out of bed in the morning, to get to church, or to stand in front of our icons and say our prayers—that is a struggle, but that is not the struggle of prayer.

The struggle of prayer is much deeper; it happens after you stand in front of the icons. It is the struggle to find God. And we, like the blind man, cannot see God passing by. We struggle with that blindness, that emptiness, that silence, that despair that says our prayers are meaningless and worthless. There is so much sin, so much distraction, and so much of ourselves in our prayers that we struggle even to say our prayers and even to believe that our prayers are being heard.

God waits, and God allows us to struggle. I often ponder on this Gospel reading. Why does Jesus allow His disciples to tell the blind man to be quiet? He could have stopped them; Jesus knew everything. Why did He allow them to go in front of Him and try to silence this blind man? We know it is not that He didn't care for the blind man, because He healed him. We know it was not that He was not touched by the blind man's illness and his plight, because His heart is full of compassion for everyone. We know it was not because He was too busy, because He stopped and listened and talked to this blind man. Why then did He allow others to try to silence him?

The answer is found in His words: "Your faith has made you whole." God knows that our prayer needs to be purified. If we understand that there is selfishness and self-love that expresses itself even in our prayer, how much more does God know how deep our pride and our self-love are and how much they infect our prayer.

So God allows us to struggle in order to purify our prayer. He allows us to struggle so that we might know our need, so that the prayer might become a cry from the very depths of our souls: Jesus, Son of God, have mercy on me! In the beginning when we pray, we pray with our mind, with our will, with our lips. So very rarely do we pray with our heart and with our soul. It is so very seldom that the cry arises from the depths of our being and consumes our being, so that our fingers and toes and knees and elbows and nose and ears and eyes and all that we are is united in our prayer, and we cry out with our whole being, "Jesus, Son of God, have mercy on me, a sinner!"

Until that prayer has consumed us, until we become the prayer and the prayer is us, until our prayer becomes the cry of a man who is drowning, who has only one hope, and that is the mercy of God—until that is our prayer, then truly we have only begun to learn how to pray. So God allows us to struggle. The Fathers say that God hides Himself, that He blankets Himself in darkness. He remains shrouded in a mist and leaves us to wander as a blind man searching for Him, groping for Him, learning that we must first unlearn, coming to know that we must first come to the place of not knowing anything, so that we might be able to say, "Jesus, Son of God, have mercy on me, a sinner."

What this means is that we must persevere. We Americans are not the persevering type. How many fads does our culture go through every year? We want something, and we want it now. If we can't get it now, we try a little bit and then give up, because we don't know how to persevere, we don't know how to endure.

God is trying to teach us perseverance. I remember when I was a young, almost-teenager, I had these visions that I would look like Arnold Schwarzenegger. I looked at myself in the mirror, and I would pretend that I was six foot three with bulging biceps. My parents for Christmas bought me an exerciser. We lived in a small house, so although I wanted a huge set of weights, they bought me a little isometric exerciser.

The idea was that when you exercised against tension, that would develop muscle strength. I didn't use it very much, because it seemed to me to be a waste of time. When I went to school I couldn't say, "I pulled the exerciser twenty times last night." I wanted to say, "I bench-pressed 200 pounds."

But the principle that works in our physical life works in our spiritual life. God allows us to come up against tension, against resistance, so that spiritual strength may be developed in us, so that we might cry out unceasingly, "Jesus, Son of God, have mercy on me," so that prayer might become the prayer of our entire being.

And if that prayer becomes united to our being, and if we persevere and endure, some day Jesus will come to us and say, "What do you want Me to do?" And we will say, "Lord, I am blind. I've searched for You all my life. Lord, I want to see You, I want to gaze upon Your beauty, I want to be enraptured with the sight of my Beloved." And the Lord will reach His hand out and say, "Child, you can now see, because your faith has made you whole."

chapter 16

What Have We Done
With What We Have Received?

Thirty-sixth Sunday after Pentecost
Matthew 25:14–30

"For the kingdom of heaven is like a man traveling to a far country, who called his own servants and delivered his goods to them. And to one he gave five talents, to another two, and to another one, to each according to his own ability; and immediately he went on a journey. Then he who had received the five talents went and traded with them, and made another five talents. And likewise he who had received two gained two more also. But he who had received one went and dug in the ground, and hid his lord's money.

"After a long time the lord of those servants came and settled accounts with them. So he who had received five talents came and brought five other talents, saying, 'Lord, you delivered to me five talents; look, I have gained five more talents besides them.' His lord said to him, 'Well done, good and faithful servant; you were faithful over a few things, I will make you ruler over many things. Enter into the joy of your lord.' He also who had received two talents came and said, 'Lord, you delivered to me two talents; look, I have gained two more talents besides them.' His lord said to him, 'Well done, good and faithful servant; you have been faithful over a few things, I will make you ruler over many things. Enter into the joy of your lord.' Then he who had received the one talent came and said, 'Lord, I knew you to be a hard man, reaping where you have not sown, and gathering where you have not scattered seed. And I was afraid,

and went and hid your talent in the ground. Look, there you have what is yours.'

"But his lord answered and said to him, 'You wicked and lazy servant, you knew that I reap where I have not sown, and gather where I have not scattered seed. So you ought to have deposited my money with the bankers, and at my coming I would have received back my own with interest. Therefore take the talent from him, and give it to him who has ten talents. For to everyone who has, more will be given, and he will have abundance; but from him who does not have, even what he has will be taken away. And cast the unprofitable servant into the outer darkness. There will be weeping and gnashing of teeth.'"

The first verse of today's epistle lesson (2 Corinthians 6:1–10) exhorts us not to receive the grace of God in vain. There is something very fearful contained in that verse: to receive the grace of God does not guarantee that the grace of God will be profitable for us. It is possible to receive the grace of God in vain. Satan entered into Judas's heart immediately after he had received the Holy Communion of Christ's Body and Blood.

That should be very frightening to us. There is no greater gift than the Holy Communion of Christ's Body and Blood. There is no way that we can receive grace more directly than to take into our bodies and our souls the very Body and Blood of Christ our God. And yet Judas received that Body and Blood, and immediately afterward, Satan entered into his heart. Judas received the grace of God in vain.

Today's Gospel lesson tells of the master who went away for a time and distributed his goods—his grace—to his servants. The first two, who had received an abundance of grace—five talents and two talents, respectively—went out and worked exceedingly hard and doubled that grace. The master commended them and promised to give them much more.

But the one who had received grace in the form of one talent received that grace in vain. For he buried the talent, then gave it back to the master—but it had not been multiplied. And the master said, "You wicked and slothful servant, I gave you my grace, but you received it in vain. You did nothing with it. Depart into the far reaches of hell and damnation, where there is weeping and gnashing of teeth."

We are the servants who have been given an abundance of grace. We will be asked to give an account of the grace we have received. That accounting will be taken, and we will not be able to say, "Well, others have done less than we," because our Lord will say that we received more. The more we receive, the more accountable we will be for what we do with it, and the more severe and strict will be our judgment.

Will we be good and faithful servants? Or will we be found to be slothful and wicked servants? Have we received the grace of God in vain, or are we showing ourselves to be faithful in using what we have received?

These are very serious questions, because although our Lord is a kind and gracious God, He is also a very exacting God. Our Lord is a God who gives us much, but also expects much from us. What have we done with what we have received? How will we answer on the Day of Judgment when we are required to give an answer?

I know that I have no defense. I have squandered so much of the grace that I have received. I should be so much further on the path than I am. Having by God's grace been put upon this path, I walk it for a time, then stray off to look at something more interesting, then come back to the path only to stray again. I am not far along the path at all, and my talents have not been multiplied.

If you face this same truth, then maybe at least you can begin to repent. You can begin to understand why we commemorate the Publican and the Pharisee, because we are the Pharisees and we need to become the publican. You can understand why we commemorate the Prodigal Son, because we are the prodigal sons who have been given the wealth of our Father, but squandered this wealth in riotous living.

You can begin to understand why during Lent we will sing, "I weep and I wail." We will say, "Woe is me, for I am a man of unclean lips and I live among people of unclean lips" (cf. Is. 6:5). You will begin to understand why we fall on our faces before God and say, "Have mercy, have mercy, have mercy."

I was talking to someone recently and made the comment, "You know, one day I will be dead." She said, "Don't say that, Father! Don't say that." I said, "Why?" She said, "I don't want to hear it. I don't want to hear that you'll be dead." And I said, "I will be, and so will you. And our bodies will be food for the worms, and our souls will have to give account."

We do not know when the master will come. The master may come for some of us today. What will we answer for the time that has been given to us? Our only answer will be, "Lord Jesus Christ, Son of God, have mercy on me, a sinner. I have squandered your grace. I have wasted the time that has been given to me. I have no talent to give back. Lord Jesus Christ, Son of God, have mercy on me, a sinner."

To whom much is given, from him much is required.

chapter 17

The Dangers of Pride

Sunday of the Publican and the Pharisee
Luke 18:10–14

"Two men went up to the temple to pray, one a Pharisee and the other a tax collector. The Pharisee stood and prayed thus with himself, 'God, I thank You that I am not like other men—extortioners, unjust, adulterers, or even as this tax collector. I fast twice a week; I give tithes of all that I possess.' And the tax collector, standing afar off, would not so much as raise his eyes to heaven, but beat his breast, saying, 'God, be merciful to me a sinner!' I tell you, this man went down to his house justified rather than the other; for everyone who exalts himself will be humbled, and he who humbles himself will be exalted."

The lesson that the Holy Church wants to give us today is clear: beware of pride. Beware of a proud thought, a proud attitude, because nothing will destroy you more quickly. Nothing will rob you of virtue more surely, nothing will take you more quickly to hell than pride.

The Pharisee was a virtuous man. He fasted twice a week, and we know that is good. He said his prayers in the morning and in the evening, and we know that is good. He gave alms, and we know that is good. But all his labor was lost, nothing he did brought any profit to his soul, because he allowed himself to become proud.

The publican was not a virtuous man. He was not a man that we would hold up to our children and say, "Be like him." But the publican received the reward of virtue because of his humility. Pride destroys; humility raises us up. Jesus ends the parable by saying,

"For everyone who exalts himself will be humbled, but he who humbles himself will be exalted."

It is easy to say that pride is an awful thing. It is easy to understand that pride will take us to hell. But it is very difficult to root out the pride that is in our souls. All of us know how subtle pride can be.

The Fathers point this out many times. They say, "You can be proud about anything. Pride can destroy anything. If you are wealthy, you can be proud of your riches, and if you are poor you can be proud of your poverty. If you get up early and say your prayers, you can be proud of how disciplined you are, and if you sleep in, you can be proud of how sinful and humble you are and how you have nothing to be proud of. You can be proud of your humility."

Pride is always subtly lurking in our souls. Pride is there when we are tempted to think or to remind others that we have done something well. Pride is there when we are angry because others do not recognize us or say the things we want them to say. The most difficult struggle of our lives is the struggle against the proud thought, against a judgmental spirit. And yet it is the most important struggle of all.

The story is told in our tradition of a monk who was not a very good monk. He slept in every morning and missed prayers. He ate too much, and he was not very diligent in anything he did. It came time for him to die, and the abbot and the brothers were concerned for his soul.

So the abbot said to the brothers, "We must do forty days' liturgy for our brother, because you know what happens to monks like him. We must work hard for the next forty days to pray for his soul, that maybe God will have mercy upon him."

The brothers were very diligent in their prayers. As they were praying for the monk's soul, the abbot had a vision. In that vision he saw that monk very close to the throne of God. Holy monks who had lived in the monastery weren't as far up as this monk. The abbot was concerned, because he didn't understand what he was seeing. He asked, "How is it, Father, that you are so close to the front? How did you attain the Kingdom when you were such a lousy monk?"

The monk said, "Father, only for one reason. Yes, it is true that I was undisciplined, I was gluttonous, and I repent of those sins. But I never judged anyone. I never harbored a thought that I was better than anyone. I never looked down and despised anyone for his sins and his struggle. And remember, Father, the words of our Lord, that with what measure you use it shall be measured to you, and with what standard of judgment you use, that very same standard God will use in judging you. Because I judged no one, God in His mercy and grace has not judged me."

Beware of the pride of the Pharisee. As we enter into Lent and begin to do things that no one else in our world is doing, beware of thinking highly of yourself. Beware of thinking poorly of those who are not doing what you are doing, because everything you gain through this Lenten struggle will be lost if you become proud.

Before we receive Holy Communion, we say a prayer in which we each confess to God and to one another that we are the chief among sinners. It's ironic, after we've gone home, how quickly we will defend ourselves when our spouse tells us we've done something wrong. How quickly we forget that we have confessed that we are the chief among sinners.

I went to a monastery once where the abbess was a very holy woman. I brought a group of lay people with me. The abbess pulled me aside and said, "Father, tell them! Please tell them now!" I said, "Mother, what do you want me to tell them?" She said, "Tell them that we're monks not because we're holy, but because we are so weak and so sinful. I don't want anyone here thinking that we are the holy ones, because that kind of thinking will destroy us."

We fast not because we're holy, but because we're so weak and sinful. We pray not because we're holy, but because we are the chief of sinners and our only hope is the mercy of God. We come to church and receive the Holy Mysteries not because we are worthy, but because we are so unworthy that we need the grace and mercy and love of God.

We are the chief of sinners. If you could see yourself as God sees you, then you would know that the only prayer that could ever come from your lips is the prayer, "God, be merciful to me, a sinner."

Pray this Holy Lent that God will open your eyes. St. John of Kronstadt says that the greatest gift God can give anyone is the gift of seeing his own sins. When I pray, I pray that God would show me my sins, but then I add an addendum: not all at once, please—just a bit at a time. I know that I would be so devastated by the sight of the depths of my sin that I would lose hope.

But each Lent, God shows us a little more. Each Lent, God takes a flashlight and walks through the house of our heart, shines His light and shows us our sin. Face the truth about yourself. Let God show you how much sin there is in your soul. And do not despair, but rather flee to God's mercy. Beat your chest, fall to the ground again and again, and cry out, "Lord Jesus Christ, Son of God, have mercy on me, a sinner."

There was a little boy who lived in a village where there was a monastery up on the hill, on the island of Cyprus. This little boy looked up and saw the monastery and thought, "What wonderful men must live up there!"

One day a monk came down and walked through the village. The little boy came up to him and said, "Father, what do you do up there all day?" The monk patted him on the head and said, "We do the same thing you do down here. We fall down and we get up again, we fall down and we get up again, we fall down and we get up again."

We fall down and say, "God, be merciful to me, a sinner." God in His mercy raises us up. We take a few steps and fall down again and say, "God, be merciful to me, a sinner." God in His mercy raises us up so that we might fall down again and say, "God, be merciful to me, a sinner."

He who walks this path of falling down and being raised up is walking the path of the publican. As Jesus reminds us at the end of the parable, two men left the temple that day, one a Pharisee and one a publican. But only the one who condemned himself, only the one who fell down before God and said, "God, be merciful to me, a sinner"—only that one received the forgiveness of his sins.

chapter 18

True Humility

Sunday of the Prodigal Son
Luke 15:11–32

Then He said: "A certain man had two sons. And the younger of them said to his father, 'Father, give me the portion of goods that falls to me.' So he divided to them his livelihood. And not many days after, the younger son gathered all together, journeyed to a far country, and there wasted his possessions with prodigal living. But when he had spent all, there arose a severe famine in that land, and he began to be in want. Then he went and joined himself to a citizen of that country, and he sent him into his fields to feed swine. And he would gladly have filled his stomach with the pods that the swine ate, and no one gave him anything.

"But when he came to himself, he said, 'How many of my father's hired servants have bread enough and to spare, and I perish with hunger! I will arise and go to my father, and will say to him, "Father, I have sinned against heaven and before you, and I am no longer worthy to be called your son. Make me like one of your hired servants."' And he arose and came to his father. But when he was still a great way off, his father saw him and had compassion, and ran and fell on his neck and kissed him. And the son said to him, 'Father, I have sinned against heaven and in your sight, and am no longer worthy to be called your son.' But the father said to his servants, 'Bring out the best robe and put it on him, and put a ring on his hand and sandals on his feet. And bring the fatted calf here and kill it, and let us eat and be merry; for this my son was dead and is alive again; he was lost and is found.' And they began to be merry.

"Now his older son was in the field. And as he came and drew near to the house, he heard music and dancing. So he called one of the servants and asked what these things meant. And he said to him, 'Your brother has come, and because he has received him safe and sound, your father has killed the fatted calf.' But he was angry and would not go in. Therefore his father came out and pleaded with him. So he answered and said to his father, 'Lo, these many years I have been serving you; I never transgressed your commandment at any time; and yet you never gave me a young goat, that I might make merry with my friends. But as soon as this son of yours came, who has devoured your livelihood with harlots, you killed the fatted calf for him.' And he said to him, 'Son, you are always with me, and all that I have is yours. It was right that we should make merry and be glad, for your brother was dead and is alive again, and was lost and is found.'"

This Gospel contains what I think is the greatest story ever to be told. We hear it every year, and every year I am amazed at the wisdom of our Lord Jesus, and at the great depth that is to be found in this story.

The first line that strikes me is found towards the beginning: "he came to himself." Here is the prodigal son, a son who has been raised in luxury and has had everything he could want—a son whose father was so gracious that he gave him half of his living.

I can remember when I was about sixteen I read this and I thought it sounded good to get half of my dad's wealth. I went and asked him if he would be like the father in the parable and split the inheritance, because I had things I wanted to buy—chiefly a new car. He looked at me like I was crazy and said, "You don't get it until I die, so forget it."

In the story we see this father, who has such grace and love that while he is living he gives the inheritance to the son. The son then goes out and has everything that he could need, and yet eventually he finds himself feeding pigs, so hungry that he is jealous of the food the pigs are eating. And then, "he came to himself."

It is the great mystery of humanity how we can be in the pigsty, sloshing around with the pigs and feeding them and jealous of what they have, and still we do not come to ourselves. What is striking to me is not that he realized where he was; it is that he was so deceived that he ended up in the pigsty, and only later did he come to himself.

We too can be so deceived by Satan and by ourselves that we cannot even see the pigsty we are living in. How is it that some wake up and see the filth that surrounds them, and the emptiness of their lives, and others do not see?

Jesus does not answer this question; He simply tells us that the prodigal son came to himself. He came to himself by remembering what real life was like. Deep in his consciousness there was a memory that he had pushed away and forgotten: the memory of life with his father. He could not push that memory away forever; it came back, and he awoke and came to himself.

We know that memory—it's a memory that all human beings have. The Fathers tell us that deep within our souls there is the memory of Paradise, of life in the Garden with God. We try to run from that memory, to push it away, but in the darkness of our own despair, the memory comes and speaks to us.

I remember the moment when I awoke, when I came to myself and realized the emptiness of my life. I remembered in the depth of my soul what humanity once enjoyed. I remembered what it was like for man to be in communion with God, and I arose and went to my Father and said, "I have sinned, I am not worthy to be called Your son, make me as one of Your hired servants."

There is another mystery in this parable. The parable ends with the prodigal son at the banquet. Many of us have experienced this in our lives. We remember when we came and the Father met us with open arms and invited us to the heavenly banquet. But if you're like me, the story does not end with the heavenly banquet.

The great tragedy of my life is that I have not been a prodigal only once, but over and over again. I come to my Father in my despair and my emptiness, in those moments of existential awareness that I am nothing, that I have nothing, and that I am in need of God. I come and weep before Him and say, "Father, I need you," and He meets me and fills me with His goodness and kills for me the fatted calf and divides His inheritance and gives it to me. And I am clothed, I take the wealth, and I go out and squander it again.

Maybe I'm smarter now, and I don't squander it in the same way that I did last time. But the mystery of my life is my ability to always invent new ways to squander wealth. We know this on a material level—we can cut up our credit cards and still go into debt. We can get new credit cards. We have an amazing ability to squander what God has given us.

Every year when this Sunday comes, I'm such a terrible sinner that I come to it thinking, "I'm so glad that we're coming to the Sunday of the Prodigal Son, because there are a few people in my church that I hope realize how prodigal they are." I always think that this year maybe this Prodigal Son Sunday will not be for me.

But in the course of my meditations every year, I see that this Sunday is for me, that I have invented a new way of squandering the richness and the wealth that God has given me, that I have been in the pigsty and have not even known it. I have been in this pigsty, looking around and seeing all the pigsties that everyone else is in and telling myself that my pigsty isn't nearly as bad as everybody else's pigsty. I used to do that when my father complained about my dirty room. I would tell him that my brother's room was far dirtier, that he should get my brother to clean up before he bothered with my almost perfectly clean room. My father would look at me and say, "This room is as much a pigsty as your brother's—clean it up!"

Every year, God comes to me and says, "Your life is as much a pigsty as everyone else's. I'm speaking to you—not to that other person, but to you. *You* have squandered, *you* must repent, and *you* must come home."

That's what Lent is all about—getting our eyes back on ourselves. We are so good at fixing everybody's life except our own. We are so good at seeing the filth in everyone else's life, and we become so used to the stench of our own that we don't notice it.

I am the prodigal son. I have squandered the riches and the wealth that God has given to me. I am in the pigsty. And I am not worthy to be called the son of God. Until we can say those words in honesty and sincerity, we have not begun to repent. We must see that we all are far from God, that we have strayed and wandered and we must return to God.

I love the words of Jesus to the church of Ephesus in the Book of Revelation: "Remember from whence you have fallen, and repent and return" (cf. Rev. 2:5). Remember: deep in your soul is the memory of communion with God. Let that memory consume you. Long only for God and for a relationship with God that is living and active. Long only to be received by God, to feed at His heavenly banquet.

chapter 19

Preparing for the Final Exam

Meatfare Sunday
Matthew 25:31–46

"When the Son of Man comes in His glory, and all the holy angels with Him, then He will sit on the throne of His glory. All the nations will be gathered before Him, and He will separate them one from another, as a shepherd divides his sheep from the goats. And He will set the sheep on His right hand, but the goats on the left. Then the King will say to those on His right hand, 'Come, you blessed of My Father, inherit the kingdom prepared for you from the foundation of the world: for I was hungry and you gave Me food; I was thirsty and you gave Me drink; I was a stranger and you took Me in; I was naked and you clothed Me; I was sick and you visited Me; I was in prison and you came to Me.' Then the righteous will answer Him, saying, 'Lord, when did we see You hungry and feed You, or thirsty and give You drink? When did we see You a stranger and take You in, or naked and clothe You? Or when did we see You sick, or in prison, and come to You?' And the King will answer and say to them, 'Assuredly, I say to you, inasmuch as you did it to one of the least of these My brethren, you did it to Me.'

"Then He will also say to those on the left hand, 'Depart from Me, you cursed, into the everlasting fire prepared for the devil and his angels: for I was hungry and you gave Me no food; I was thirsty and you gave Me no drink; I was a stranger and you did not take Me in, naked and you did not clothe Me, sick and in prison and you did not visit Me.' Then they also will answer Him, saying, 'Lord, when did we see You hungry

or thirsty or a stranger or naked or sick or in prison, and did not minister to You?' Then He will answer them, saying, 'Assuredly, I say to you, inasmuch as you did not do it to one of the least of these, you did not do it to Me.' And these will go away into everlasting punishment, but the righteous into eternal life."

I remember when I was in school, especially when I was starting out in college, the professors made a big point of handing out the syllabus on the first day of class. The syllabus would contain all the assignments and readings that had to be done and by when.

The professors would always make sure to point out when the exams were. At the beginning of every class they would stress the exam, and tell us what was going to be on it, when it would be held, and how much the exam was worth in terms of the overall grade.

We would sit there and feel fear. Here it was the first day of class, and we were being reminded that there was an exam. In the first couple of years of college the professors would remind us of that exam over and over, saying, "Remember, you're going to be tested on this. Remember there is an exam, and you should be studying now for the exam that is to come."

Some friends of mine thought that the idea of college was to play, and did not take seriously the assignments and the readings for the coming exam. As I was down in the cafeteria studying with all my books, they would be sitting there talking to each other and having lots of fun. I would sit in a cubby away from them, and I can remember them looking at me and laughing, "Look at that guy over there studying!"

But I was more afraid of the exam than I was of their laughter. I endured their laughter as I sat and studied, and I said to myself, "We'll see who's laughing on exam day." The exam came and I was prepared, because I had studied.

I can remember the fear in their eyes on the day before the exam, when all of a sudden they remembered that the reason they were at college was to learn. They would walk into the exam with rings under their eyes because they had studied all night. I'd had a good night's sleep and was wide awake, because I had been studying the entire semester for the exam, and they had only studied the night before.

Jesus and the Holy Church stand before us today and say to us, "There is an exam. There is a final exam that each and every one of us will have to take. We will have to stand by ourselves in front of the Judge of all mankind and give an account for every word we have spoken, for every deed we have done, and for every deed we have not done. We will have to give an account for how we have spent our time." And that exam will be worth the entire grade.

It's easy for us to forget that there is an exam. We live in a world in which everyone tells us, "Live! Be free! Don't worry about such things! Just have fun today, that's all that matters." We Christians pass our time in this world as I did in the cafeteria, sitting and studying while many around us laugh and mock, because we know that there is an exam.

It's very fearful to hear the words of our Gospel: "When the Son of Man comes . . ." Now I would have preferred Jesus to say, "*If* the Son of Man comes." But Jesus says, "*When* the Son of Man comes." When He comes in all His glory with all His angels, and when the nations are gathered before Him, then the books will be opened and the judgment will be made.

The Book of Revelation (6:15–17) shows us a picture of this great and final day. All the nations will be gathered together before the throne of Christ, and many will say, "Let the mountains fall upon us and cover us. Let the rocks open up that we might hide, for who will spare us from this great and awful day?"

Then comes the line that strikes fear into my soul: "For who can endure the wrath of the Lamb?" Lambs are not generally characterized by their wrath. When you think of a lamb, you think of something that is sweet and innocent and playful. You never think of something that is full of anger and wrath.

Yet on that great and final day, many will cry, "Who will spare us from the wrath of the Lamb?" When the Son of Man comes, each and every one of us will appear before Him, and we will have to answer for what we have done.

Some time ago I saw a cartoon in which two men went out

jogging. The cartoon began as they're getting ready, and one of them is putting huge cages on his legs. The other one is laughing and making fun of him—"Can you imagine wearing those things to go jogging?"

They start jogging, and it's so hard for the one with the cages on his legs to jog. He has to keep his legs centered so he doesn't trip. The other one's having a great time, laughing at the one with the cages, saying, "Can you believe such an idiot would wear those cages?"

In the last picture, a pack of dogs comes out of the forest. The one with the cages is fine, because the dogs cannot bite his legs. The one that doesn't have the cages feels the dogs devouring his legs. The one with the cages looks over and says, "They don't look so funny now, do they?"

All the things we do—the fasting that we begin tomorrow, the prayer and vigil-keeping and almsgiving that we will do during Lent, the repentance and confession—look so silly in the eyes of the world. But on that great and final Day of Judgment, they won't look so silly, because they will have prepared us to stand before that great and awesome Judge and give an account. They will have prepared us for entrance into the eternal Kingdom.

chapter 20

Turning in the Right Direction

Cheesefare Sunday
Matthew 6:14–21

> *"For if you forgive men their trespasses, your heavenly Father will also forgive you. But if you do not forgive men their trespasses, neither will your Father forgive your trespasses.*
>
> *"Moreover, when you fast, do not be like the hypocrites, with a sad countenance. For they disfigure their faces that they may appear to men to be fasting. Assuredly, I say to you, they have their reward. But you, when you fast, anoint your head and wash your face, so that you do not appear to men to be fasting, but to your Father who is in the secret place; and your Father who sees in secret will reward you openly.*
>
> *"Do not lay up for yourselves treasures on earth, where moth and rust destroy and where thieves break in and steal; but lay up for yourselves treasures in heaven, where neither moth nor rust destroys and where thieves do not break in and steal. For where your treasure is, there your heart will be also."*

I remember something that happened to me when I was first playing basketball. I was in the fifth or sixth grade and had joined a team, and it was a very exciting time for me—the first time I was going to play organized ball.

I didn't start out on the first string; I was second or third string. I can remember sitting on the bench waiting to get in and being so excited about being able to play in a basketball game. Finally the coach said it was my time to enter the game. I was ready to play, it was the moment I had waited for.

The ball was out of bounds, I remember, and I was guarding

my man, and I could tell that the other player was going to pass it to my man. So when the pass came I jumped in front, grabbed the ball, began to dribble, and headed right for the hoop. It was amazing, because all the players on the other team sort of moved out of my way. Everybody started screaming in the whole place, and I was sure that I was a star, that I was the greatest. They weren't even guarding me because they knew there was no point.

Everybody was screaming, and as I got close to the basket, I began to distinguish the words that were being screamed. I was hearing, "No, no, you're going the wrong way! It's the wrong hoop! We're going the other way!" As the ball exited my hand to go into the basket, I saw the faces of all my teammates cast down, and the other team was so excited because I had scored for them.

What happened to me in that basketball game often happens to us in the spiritual life. It is easy for us to be confused, to be deceived, to be so sure of ourselves that we interpret everything as meaning that we are doing it right, when in reality we are doing it wrong.

That is why this is one of my favorite days of the year, because tomorrow we begin the Great Fast. The fast is the greatest time of the year. It's a time of great rejoicing, because for the next forty days we get to distinguish the words that are being screamed. During the next forty days we are given insights into how we are living, and in what direction we are proceeding.

We all will find that we have been shooting at the wrong baskets. Many of us think that we are doing things right, and we must be shown that we are doing things very wrong. Great Lent is given to us so that we might see ourselves, so that we might take stock of what is truly going on inside of us, so that we might repent, so that we might stop before we score for the other team. Satan hates this time of the year.

Orthodox Christians tend to love Lent. Wherever I go they all say the same thing to me: "I can't wait for Lent to be here." We rejoice in being shown where we are wrong. We don't live our lives hoping that someone will tell us that we are doing something right. As hard and as painful as it is, we hope that people will show us where we're doing things wrong. The saints' greatest fear was that someone would say something positive about them. They were so happy when people said negative things.

A priest friend of mine has many good people in his parish who are very supportive. He also has a few people who think that he is the worst priest in the world. I talked to him once just after this latter group had shared with him all the things that he had done wrong, and how they were going to find a new spiritual father, because certainly anybody was better than he was. He said, "Thank God some people in my parish have got it right." I said, "Yes, isn't it wonderful when people support you?" He said, "No, Father, they're the ones who have it wrong. Thank God there are at least some in my parish who understand that I'm good for nothing."

He is truly Orthodox. Those of us who struggle with our pride would sit all day and say, "This person thinks I'm good, this person thinks I'm good, those people don't know what they're talking about." This Orthodox priest said, "Thank God for those who have said bad things about me, because they're the ones who have it right, and I need to repent."

Great Lent is given to us so that we might repent, so that we might see our sins, so that we might find out what is wrong with us. When I go to a doctor, I don't say, "Doctor, tell me everything that is good about me. Tell me everything that's working." And the doctor doesn't say, "This is really working well, and this is really working well. Half of your body is just doing wonderfully!"

When I go to the doctor I say, "Doctor, these are the symptoms—what's wrong with me?" My doctor says, "This is wrong, and this is wrong, and this is wrong." I don't get angry at him and say, "How dare you say those things about me! I know people who think I'm doing great!" I say, "Thank you," and then, "How can we fix it?" The doctor says, "I'm not quite sure. But you can try this for a while and we'll see if it works."

Why don't we do the same thing in the spiritual life? I have a good friend who, before he goes to confession, goes around to each member of his family and says, "I need to go to confession—can you write my list for me? Tell me everything I need to confess, because I know I don't see it myself." He comes to confession with the list that's written by others, and then he adds all the other sins that he can see.

He wants to repent. He wants to be shown where he's failing, so that he can ask forgiveness, so that he can change. That's why Great Lent has been given to us.

The Synaxarion points out that the time of Great Lent is approximately ten percent of the year—a tithe. The Synaxarion says that we should be fasting and praying and repenting every day of the year, because we're such terrible sinners. But we're weak and we're not ready for that kind of spiritual labor.

Now the Church and God come to you and ask for a tithe of your time: forty days to think about nothing but your soul and what you are doing wrong. Forty days to deny yourself pleasure, to say no to what you want, and yes to what is good for you. Forty days to humble yourself, to abase yourself. Forty days to center your thoughts and attention on your spiritual life and how you need to change.

Everyone who's been through Lent knows how easy it is to fail at Lent. On Cheesefare Sunday everyone says, "I'm going to have a good Lent, it's going to be different this year." And we get to the end of Lent and say, "What happened? How did I blow it?"

Let me fill you in on a few ways that Satan is going to try to ruin your Lent. We read it in today's Gospel. First of all, he's going to try to get you to pay more attention to the sins and failings of others than to your own. He's going to incite your curiosity. Satan is the most curious of all beings. He's going to want you to be more interested in the lives of others than in your own.

He's going to attempt to get you angry and bitter with resentment over the wrongs that have been done to you. So Jesus in our Gospel says, "Forgive." At Vespers on this Sunday in our rite of forgiveness we will ask each other for forgiveness and we will say, "It's over, it's all forgiven."

Satan will attempt to get you to worry about what other people are thinking and saying about you. He may get you thinking that you're a great person, so you have to tell everybody around you what you're doing. Many of us are very good at broadcasting to everyone the spiritual struggles that we're having. We're good at reminding people that we're fasting: "Oh, I can't do that tonight because I have to spend four hours in prayer." Satan can distract us into worrying about presenting ourselves positively.

But Satan can also distract us by getting us to worry about negative things people say. How many people have stopped their fast because "I don't want someone to know that I'm fasting." They say it in a very pious way—"I don't want to broadcast that I'm fasting, I don't want to be proud"—but really what they're saying is, "I don't want anyone to look down on me because I'm fasting. I don't want people to know that I take my spiritual life seriously, because they won't understand, so I'm not going to fast today." See how subtle sin can be? We're not concerned about our humility, we're concerned about what other people think.

Satan will try to make us irritable. Most of us get irritable when we fast. Satan will try to distract us. Forty days is a long time for us to be focused on anything. Be very careful.

There are great rewards promised to those who fast. There are great blessings given to those who take this time seriously. On the Feast of Pascha, St. John Chrysostom will say, "Come one, come all, you who came at the first and you who came at the eleventh hour, because the meal is all ready." Thank God that, in His grace, even when we fall He is there to receive us. But from a human standpoint, if we come at the first and endure, there is so much more that we will receive than if we come at the eleventh hour.

So let us enter the fast with joy and thanksgiving. Thank God that right now He is screaming at you, "No, no! You're going the wrong way! That's the wrong basket!" Thank God that He and all the saints are there to remind us that the hoop is at the other end of the court, and we need to change direction and go that way.

chapter 21

Freedom in Christ

First Sunday of Lent, Sunday of Orthodoxy
John 1:43–51

The following day Jesus wanted to go to Galilee, and He found Philip and said to him, "Follow Me." Now Philip was from Bethsaida, the city of Andrew and Peter. Philip found Nathanael and said to him, "We have found Him of whom Moses in the law, and also the prophets, wrote—Jesus of Nazareth, the son of Joseph." And Nathanael said to him, "Can anything good come out of Nazareth?" Philip said to him, "Come and see."

Jesus saw Nathanael coming toward Him, and said of him, "Behold, an Israelite indeed, in whom is no deceit!" Nathanael said to Him, "How do You know me?" Jesus answered and said to him, "Before Philip called you, when you were under the fig tree, I saw you." Nathanael answered and said to Him, "Rabbi, You are the Son of God! You are the King of Israel!" Jesus answered and said to him, "Because I said to you, 'I saw you under the fig tree,' do you believe? You will see greater things than these." And He said to him, "Most assuredly, I say to you, hereafter you shall see heaven open, and the angels of God ascending and descending upon the Son of Man."

Today we come to the first feast of the Lenten season: the Triumph of Orthodoxy, in which we celebrate the restoration of the icons to the Church. At the end of today's Liturgy, we announce to the world: "This is the faith of the Prophets, this is the faith of the Apostles, this is the faith of the Fathers, this is the faith that has conquered the universe."

I find it interesting that this day in which we rejoice in the faith, this day of celebration and victory, comes during these holy days in which we are fasting. God doesn't do anything by mistake or without purpose. Why is it that God chose this Sunday, the first Sunday of the fast, to be the day on which the icons were restored to the Church? Why is it that this Sunday is the day on which we celebrate the triumph of Orthodoxy?

If we had been setting this up, we probably would have picked a day during Pascha. Maybe the Sunday after Pascha, when we've been eating meat all week long, and we can have a real feast after service and celebrate by gorging ourselves on all the foods that we like. But God chose something different. The fact that He chose this Sunday to be the triumph of Orthodoxy says some very important things to us.

Why do we fast? I was talking to someone about the fast, and he said, "I can't believe that all of your people go without meat for forty days. Father, you have to understand, I'm a steak-and-potatoes man. My idea of heaven is a room filled with filet mignon." I looked at him and said, "Listen to what you just said. Your idea of heaven is a room filled with filet mignon. Do you think that maybe your idea of heaven needs a bit of improvement? It's too much concerned with the things of this world. If heaven to you is eating steak, then something is very wrong with your understanding of the Gospel and of what it means to be saved."

Of course he said, "I didn't mean it literally," and I said, "You used the words. The fact that you chose to use those words reflects something very deep in your heart. It reflects the fact that you have lowered your view of heaven, and when you think about good things, you think about serving your belly. When you think about the best of times, you think about eating and drinking. When you think about heaven, you don't even think about God."

What is heaven? Heaven is not sitting down to a full-course meal of filet mignon. According to the Scriptures, heaven is being in the presence of God. In heaven there will be no eating or drinking such as we know now, and there will be no marrying and giving in marriage. In heaven there will be no lights and no sun, because as the Book of Revelation says to us, the Lamb Himself will be our food, and our drink, and our light (Rev. 21:23). In heaven we will feed on God and drink of God; we will praise God and find great joy simply by being in His presence.

Of course, when you say that to many people in the world today, they say, "That doesn't sound like heaven to me." I've said that to people, and they've commented on how boring that would be. "You mean in heaven it's just going to be one liturgy that never stops? Don't you get to do something fun in heaven?"

All of these things show how far we are removed from understanding what it means to be a Christian, what it means to be human, what we were created to be and to do. We were not created to live off the dead flesh of animals. Adam did not eat meat in the Garden. He lived in communion with God. He was complete and healthy, and he was filled with great joy. Something happened at the Fall. In the Garden of Eden, Adam's spirit was in control of his body, and his body served his spirit. At the Fall, Adam was reversed, and his body ruled his spirit. "For dust you are, and to dust you shall return" (Gen. 3:19). The Fathers say that after the Fall Adam, who was intended to look up and receive from God, lowered his hands and his gaze and looked to the things of this world to satisfy, to be for him what God had once been.

The end result of this reversal is bondage. We are in bondage. Everyone always seems to be so tired during the first week of Lent, because they have cut back on how much they are eating and drinking, and everybody is moping around and has no energy. We think we are such strong people, we think that we are capable of doing anything, but you take food and drink away from us for eight or nine hours, and we are good for nothing. We get irritable and impatient. We are enslaved to our passions and the demands of our flesh.

Christ has come to set us free from bondage to our passions and to the things of this world, so that we can be like the Apostle Paul, who said, "I have learned in whatever state I am, to be content: I know how to be abased, and I know how to abound. Everywhere and in all things I have learned both to be full and to be hungry, both to abound and to suffer need. I can do all things through Christ who strengthens me" (Phil. 4:11–13).

It's not wrong for us to eat meat and dairy products. It's not wrong for us to eat and be full. What is so tragic is that if you take a few things away from us, we grumble and complain and become angry and irritable, we have no patience, we snap at our children, we speak angrily to our spouses, we are sullen. That is the tragedy.

Christ has come to be everything for us. Christ has come to set us free so that we can be happy and joyful when we have everything and when we have nothing, so that we can rejoice and have a feast in the middle of our fast and at the end of our fast. He is teaching us to say with the Apostle Paul: "I can do all things through Christ who strengthens me." It's very easy to say that when our bodies are full, when we have everything. But the truth is revealed when we are hungry, when we lose everything, when we are in pain.

So today we triumph and celebrate. We celebrate because we know that the faith has been given to us whole and intact. We celebrate because we know that God became a man, that God took on the same flesh and blood that you and I have—that God was hungry, thirsty, and in great pain, that on the Cross God was smitten with an agony that you and I cannot comprehend.

In His agony and pain and thirst and hunger, God has shown us the triumph of faith, because He hung on the Cross. Even as He cried out those words of great agony, "I thirst," and, "My God, my God, why have You forsaken Me?" He also cried out those words of deepest love: "Father, forgive them, for they know not what they do." Those words of deep concern and compassion: "Woman, behold your son. Son, behold your mother" (cf. Matt. 27:46; Luke 23:34; John 19:26–28). In His hour of greatest need and suffering, in His hour of great thirst and hunger, in His hour of abject poverty, when even the garments had been stripped off Him, and the soldiers were at the foot of the Cross auctioning them off, and all His friends had abandoned Him—in that hour in which He had nothing, our Lord stretched out His hands and embraced the whole world with His love and care.

That is our triumph, that is our boast, and that is our joy. We can have everything when we have nothing, because we have learned that God is all we need, that God is our joy and our life, that Jesus is the very breath we breathe. Jesus is every heartbeat. Jesus is our drink and Jesus is our food.

chapter 22

Healing the Paralysis of the Soul

Second Sunday of Lent, St. Gregory Palamas
Mark 2:1–12

And again He entered Capernaum after some days, and it was heard that He was in the house. Immediately many gathered together, so that there was no longer room to receive them, not even near the door. And He preached the word to them. Then they came to Him, bringing a paralytic who was carried by four men. And when they could not come near Him because of the crowd, they uncovered the roof where He was. So when they had broken through, they let down the bed on which the paralytic was lying.

When Jesus saw their faith, He said to the paralytic, "Son, your sins are forgiven you." And some of the scribes were sitting there and reasoning in their hearts, "Why does this Man speak blasphemies like this? Who can forgive sins but God alone?"

But immediately, when Jesus perceived in His spirit that they reasoned thus within themselves, He said to them, "Why do you reason about these things in your hearts? Which is easier, to say to the paralytic, 'Your sins are forgiven you,' or to say, 'Arise, take up your bed and walk'? But that you may know that the Son of Man has power on earth to forgive sins"—He said to the paralytic, "I say to you, arise, take up your bed, and go to your house." Immediately he arose, took up the bed, and went out in the presence of them all, so that all were amazed and glorified God, saying, "We never saw anything like this!"

There are many things we can learn from this story. We learn that to get to Jesus requires work. Many of us, if we had been coming to see Jesus and had seen the crowd that was gathered out-side that house, would have said, "We'll come back another day. It's too much work; there's no way we can do it."

The spiritual life is a life of struggle. It is a life in which we face obstacles, and we must pursue and persevere and overcome those obstacles in order to make it to Jesus. It is obvious why the Holy Church would appoint this lesson to be read in the middle of Lent, because Lent is a struggle. There are many obstacles that come our way, and there are many times when we are tempted to say, "Why am I trying? What's the point? I'll never make it. Why should I go through all this only to fail anyway? It would be easier if I didn't try."

We are reminded of the importance of struggle and that God will bless our struggle. How did the paralytic's friends think of cut-ting through the roof and lowering him down? Jesus does not say, but it is not too much to guess that this idea was suggested to them by God Himself. As we struggle to come towards God, God is not uninterested in our struggle. Jesus, even as He was in the house teaching, was aware of those on the outside, and He was aiding them in their struggle to get to Him.

It's a great mystery: we are struggling to get to God, and some-times it feels as if it is all our labor, we are doing everything. But when we get to God, we find out that it is not so much that we came to God, but rather that God drew us to Himself, and the energy and the wisdom and the perseverance were gifts from God.

We live this mystery each Lent, because we struggle during Lent, there are many obstacles, and we feel at times as if we are doing everything. We fall down before God and say, "Why aren't you help-ing me more? Why do I have to do everything? Why do you make everything so hard?" At that same time that we are asking God those questions, He is aiding us. He is beside us, and it is His grace that is sustaining us.

We see this picture of the four young men, and the man who was so sick that he could do nothing himself. Can you imagine what it was like to be that man, lying on that bed, paralyzed from the neck down, wanting to get to Christ and unable to do anything by himself? Can you imagine the looks of all those who were in the home as the man came down on his mat? How vulnerable he must have felt, how his own sickness must have been magnified in his eyes! Here he is in the middle of the room with all eyes upon him and he can do nothing, because he is paralyzed. He lies there, helpless, unable to do anything.

Jesus looks at him and says words that are very deep in meaning, words that may have surprised the paralytic. Jesus does not say to him, "Arise and walk." We know that Jesus can say this, because He says it to so many throughout the Gospels. But to this one Jesus says, "Son, your sins are forgiven." Why "your sins are forgiven"? Why not "arise and walk"?

The Fathers say that Jesus saw the reason for this man's paralysis. There are some sicknesses—not all—that are caused by our own sin. This man was paralyzed because of the sins he had committed. Before he could be healed, he first needed to be forgiven. In this story, there is therefore revealed one very important truth: sin always paralyzes those who commit it.

We have an idea that has been fed to us by Satan that sin is fun, that sin is enjoyment and excitement and the opportunity to receive what we desire, and that somehow God stands in the way and says, "No, you can't do that because I don't want you to have any fun. I'm going to stand in your way, because I want you to be miserable and unfulfilled and lacking in things." We think that sin will bring us freedom, and God is the one who is paralyzing us, limiting our ability to move.

In fact, the opposite is true. It is not sin that frees, it is sin that paralyzes. Anyone who has struggled with sin knows that sin comes to you seeming so innocent. It invites you in, and it presents itself with a thousand reasons why it's okay this time for you to do it. So you commit the sin, and all of a sudden you find yourself trapped. The next time the sin is easier to commit, and it is like a spider's web: the more we struggle, the more entrapped we become, until we find ourselves unable to move.

For most of us, the paralysis is not in our bodies. Rather, it is the paralysis of the soul. When you sin, you find it difficult to pray. The more you give yourself over to sin, the more difficult it is for you to pray, to believe, to know joy, to feel peace, to see or hear anything that is spiritual. The things that used to make sense and bring joy all of a sudden seem silly and burdensome. It is because your soul has become paralyzed.

As we struggle this Lent against sin, we see today the true nature of sin. You see what sin has done to you: how any movement away from God has brought paralysis into your soul. You see yourself as lying in front of Jesus, unable to move. As we see in this story the necessity of struggle and the true nature of sin, we see also in this story where victory is to be found.

It is Christ who grants victory. One of the ironies of life is that we have inflated images of our ability to handle our own lives. Even as most of our soul is trapped in the spider's web of sin, we still feel that we can set ourselves free if we only work harder, if we only struggle more. This, too, is a lie of Satan, because we cannot free ourselves.

Lent is given to us not for victory, but so that we might see our failures. Everybody begins Lent by saying, "We're going to have a great Lent." Two weeks into Great Lent we all stumble into church and we have fallen, we have failed. We stand around with our heads hanging low and we think, "How in two weeks could I have made so many mistakes? How could I have blown it as much as I have?"

We cannot save ourselves, but Christ can set us free. So we lie on our beds and say, "Jesus, Son of God, have mercy on me, a sinner." We throw ourselves at the feet of Christ and say, "We cannot save ourselves. We have tried and we have failed—Jesus, Son of God, have mercy on me, a sinner."

It is then, when we have realized how much we are in need of Christ, that Christ comes and sets us free. The great irony is that having been set free by Christ, we begin to think that we can do it by ourselves again. We run to another spider's web, or even go back to the very same sin that trapped us in the beginning. So we come over and over again to God, lying on that bed, saying, "Jesus, Son of God, have mercy on me, a sinner."

The amazing thing about God is that He never gets tired of setting us free. Have you noticed that? God is so wonderful and so loving that He never gets tired of reaching His hand down and delivering us. He never pushes us away and says, "I've had enough of you; you've failed one too many times. I'm done with you, it's over, I'm going to go and find Myself better material." God's love is so wonderful that He receives us and frees us, and pours His grace out into our hearts and our lives—over and over again.

chapter 23

The Paradox of the Cross

Third Sunday of Lent, Veneration of the Cross
Mark 8:34—9:1

When He had called the people to Himself, with His disciples also, He said to them, "Whoever desires to come after Me, let him deny himself, and take up his cross, and follow Me. For whoever desires to save his life will lose it, but whoever loses his life for My sake and the gospel's will save it. For what will it profit a man if he gains the whole world, and loses his own soul? Or what will a man give in exchange for his soul? For whoever is ashamed of Me and My words in this adulterous and sinful generation, of him the Son of Man also will be ashamed when He comes in the glory of His Father with the holy angels." And He said to them, "Assuredly, I say to you that there are some standing here who will not taste death till they see the kingdom of God present with power."

A great paradox is presented in this Gospel: the paradox of the cross. The cross is an instrument of torture. It is such an awful weapon that it has been outlawed, and no crucifixions take place in our day and age. Even in the time of Constantine the Great, it was made illegal for anyone to be hung upon a cross. It is an emblem of torture, disgrace, and shame. It is the sign of pain, of agony, of everything that could be wrong. Yet this cross, this sign of all that is wrong with us as human beings—this cross is for us life-giving. This cross is a sign of rejoicing and victory. This cross is our salvation.

If we understand that, then we can understand what Jesus has to say to us in this Gospel: "Whoever wishes to be My disciple, let him take up his cross, deny himself, and follow Me." For those who lived before the victory of Christ on Golgotha and the empty tomb, for the disciples who heard that word, it was a great mystery. What did Jesus mean, "let him take up his cross and follow Me"? How can we take up pain and torture and suffering and self-denial? How can that be what it means to follow God?

Just before Jesus announces this great mystery, He has told His disciples: "I am going to the cross and I will be treated shamefully and I will suffer and I will die." Peter speaks for the disciples and says, "Far be it from You, Lord. Such things are not fitting for God Incarnate." How could God be impaled on an emblem of shame and torture? Jesus looks at Peter and says in the presence of all His disciples (because Peter was speaking for all the disciples, who shared his mindset): "Get behind Me, Satan. For I say unto you, if any man wishes to come after Me, let him take up his cross, let him deny himself and follow Me" (cf. Mark 8:31–33).

What a hard saying that was for the disciples, to know that in order to follow Christ each one of them would have to suffer, that every one of them, save one, would be nailed upon a cross or in some way suffer the death of a martyr. Yet our Lord makes no mistake. He goes on and says, "For whoever desires to save his life will lose it, but whoever loses his life for My sake and the gospel's will save it"—words that are even more mysterious.

For those who lived before the greatest demonstration of this spiritual principle, how confusing this must have been. The disciples had no frame of reference in which to think about these things. "What does He mean? We've been taught from the day we were born that we must take care of ourselves. We have within us the desire for life, which is so overwhelming and controlling that we flee from death. We will do anything to escape the torturous nature of death.

"Yet Jesus is saying to us that we must be committed to losing our life, that we must be open to giving everything up. Not just our possessions, for we have heard His words that we must sell all that we have and give it to the poor and follow Him—that was hard enough. We have heard Him say to people that they have to leave behind their family and their employment and everything they have, and that was hard enough. But now He says we must leave behind our very life. We must count our life as nothing. We must embrace our death. We must give every moment to God, so that we might live."

How the disciples must have been confused! Their entire world collapsed. We know that they had followed Jesus because they thought that He was the Messiah, that He was going to set His people free—isn't that what all the prophets had pronounced? And now He was telling them that His way was the way of the cross, His way was the way of death to self; the victory and the liberty that He was giving to them would demand from them everything.

There was one disciple who could not abide this teaching. The Fathers say that it was at this time that Judas turned his back on Christ. Judas decided the way of the cross was too hard. The other eleven, not knowing what Jesus meant, decided in their hearts that they would follow Him even to death. They walked the path of the cross. They didn't walk it perfectly, and there were times when the demands of the cross were too much for them and they fled. Their leader, the one who had said, "Jesus, no," even fled so far as to deny Christ three times. But in their hearts, even though they were weak and made mistakes, they walked the way of the cross.

We who are so many centuries removed have it much easier. I'm glad that God didn't choose me to be alive when He was alive on earth, because I know that in my weakness I would have been Judas; I could not have understood, my faith is far too weak. I would have said, "It's too much," and I would have turned my back on my Lord.

The Lord is so kind to us, so gracious and so loving, because He knows how hard this is. He knows it's true, because He's God, and yet He knows how hard it is for our humanity, because as man He Himself struggled in the Garden. He Himself cried out, "O My Father, if it is possible, let this cup pass from Me; nevertheless, not as I will, but as You *will*" (Matt. 26:39).

Our Lord knew how we need to be saved, He knew what was required of each one of us—that we must die to our ego, to our self, to our desires, to everything. We must die to self in order to live. He knew the only hope for humanity was this message of death. He did not stay up there in heaven far removed from us. He came down and became one of us. He knew that we would find it hard to believe that our death is our life, because the paradox is too great for our feeble minds. So before He called anyone to walk the way of the cross, God first walked the way of the cross Himself.

God said, "He who would save his life will lose it, and he who will lose his life will save it, and I know you don't believe Me, and I know it's too hard for you. So watch Me, because I am going to the cross, and I will lose everything. My loss will be so intense that on the cross I will cry, 'My God, My God, why have You forsaken Me?' On the cross I will give up My life.

"I will do it first, and I will find life through death, so that you weak, feeble-minded men and women who cannot believe will see Me, and will see that I am speaking the truth. I have passed through death to life, and all you have to do is follow Me, and die with Me, so that I might give you life: life more abundant, more full and more rich than you can even imagine."

Isn't God wonderful? How many people in this world tell us to do things that are good for us that they themselves do not do? My father told me to eat my spinach, but I never saw him eat spinach in his life. It was hard for me to believe that spinach was good for me if my dad wouldn't eat it himself.

But God has done everything He asks of us. He was already God, He had no sin, there was nothing in Him that deserved death. So that I might understand, so that I might believe, He, the giver of life, died. He, the giver of every good thing, endured the cross, not for Himself, but for me.

As we venerate the cross in our midst, let us remind our hearts of Jesus, and let us see what He has done so that we might do the same, so that through our death we might find life eternal.

chapter 24

Drawing on the Strength of Christ

Fourth Sunday of Lent, St. John of the Ladder
Mark 9:16–30

*And He asked the scribes, "What are you discussing with
them?" Then one of the crowd answered and said, "Teacher, I
brought You my son, who has a mute spirit. And wherever it
seizes him, it throws him down; he foams at the mouth, gnashes
his teeth, and becomes rigid. So I spoke to Your disciples, that
they should cast it out, but they could not." He answered him
and said, "O faithless generation, how long shall I be with you?
How long shall I bear with you? Bring him to Me."*

*Then they brought him to Him. And when he saw Him,
immediately the spirit convulsed him, and he fell on the ground
and wallowed, foaming at the mouth. So He asked his father,
"How long has this been happening to him?" And he said, "From
childhood. And often he has thrown him both into the fire and
into the water to destroy him. But if You can do anything, have
compassion on us and help us." Jesus said to him, "If you can
believe, all things are possible to him who believes." Immediately the father of the child cried out and said with tears, "Lord,
I believe; help my unbelief!"*

*When Jesus saw that the people came running together, He
rebuked the unclean spirit, saying to it, "Deaf and dumb spirit,
I command you, come out of him and enter him no more!"
Then the spirit cried out, convulsed him greatly, and came out
of him. And he became as one dead, so that many said, "He is
dead." But Jesus took him by the hand and lifted him up, and
he arose.*

And when He had come into the house, His disciples asked

Him privately, "Why could we not cast it out?" So He said to them, "This kind can come out by nothing but prayer and fasting." Then they departed from there and passed through Galilee, and He did not want anyone to know it.

I remember when I was a boy, every summer the carnival would come to town. We would go on the various rides, and my parents would give us a certain amount of money that we could spend, and it was a lot of fun.

One year there was a new attraction at the carnival. It was a tall, slender pole; at the top was a silver bell and in the front was a big pad. Next to the pad was a big sledgehammer. On the pole there were lines with words: the first line said "Wimp," at the next line it said "Almost," and then at the top it said "He-man."

I was about eleven or twelve years old at the time. I decided that it was time to make my mark; I was going to show the world that I was a he-man. I watched other young boys go up and be classified as wimps, and I laughed and laughed. "Look at those weaklings," I thought to myself. I even said to my brother, "Can you believe how weak these boys are? Wait until we show them what real men are made of."

It came my turn and I sauntered up. The man said to me, "Are you sure you can do this?" I said very loud, "Of course. It will be easy." He looked at me again, up and down, and asked, "Are you really sure you can do this?" (knowing what I did not know), and I said again, "Of course." So he said, "Well, go ahead and try."

I walked over to that sledgehammer, feeling so confident as I went to pick it up. I could barely get it off the ground. I could not get it over my shoulder. There was no way I was going to swing this thing. I tried to keep the scraps of my pride together as I walked over and dropped it on the pad. I didn't even register as a wimp.

I walked home and said, "I'm done with the carnival. I'm never going to show my face in the world again." Of course my brother walked behind me the whole way, laughing and laughing.

If you understand that story, then you understand how the disciples felt in this Gospel reading. This man came to the disciples with a son who was demon-possessed. The disciples said, "Hey, not a problem, we can take care of this. You don't need to bother Jesus with this one. We've been with him now for a long time—over two years—and this one we can handle." But they could not handle it. They did not even register as wimps. Why?

Of course it is a question that we ask ourselves, because we are like the disciples. How many of us thought that we could make it through Great Lent and at the end register as one of those he-men? The Church gave us the sledgehammer of fasting on Clean Monday. We walked up and said, "We're going to swing this sledgehammer and we're going to destroy our passions!"

Now the fourth Sunday of Lent is here, and we have barely registered as wimps on the scale. Many of us have found that this sledgehammer that looked so easy is a lot harder to carry than we thought. If we haven't struggled with fasting from food, then we have struggled with fasting from evil words, or anger, or lustful thoughts, or avarice, or slander, or deception—with all of these we have struggled and we have barely raised that sledgehammer.

Every year I think I'm going to breeze through Lent. Every year I get to this Sunday and realize that I have done so little, and I am so weak. As we have taken what little strength we have and used this hammer called fasting against our passions, we have broken very little of our passions' hold on our lives.

We set out this Lent saying that we were going to have a Lent without anger. Even in the first week we were speaking angry words. We said we were going to pray every morning, and we were not going to oversleep even once. Clean Week wasn't even over before we had pushed the snooze button four times and were running late. We said that we were going to be generous, that we were not going to spend our time taking care of ourselves, but we were going to devote ourselves this Lent to taking care of others. All of a sudden we look back and see that most of our energy has been directed toward ourselves, that we are filled with selfishness.

So we, like the disciples, have been humbled by the fast. We come back to Jesus and say, "Lord, if You can, will You heal me? If You can, will You break that part of me that I cannot break?" My heart is like granite, and I have nothing but a little toy hammer. I bang it against the granite of my heart and my heart does not break. It's the hammer that breaks. I feel as if the hammer of my effort has been broken, and my heart is as hard as it ever was. We come to Jesus and say, "Break the hardness of my heart."

A year after I had thoroughly embarrassed myself at the carnival, the carnival came back to town. We were all excited again, and we got our money and went to the carnival. I walked in and saw the long pole with the sledgehammer and the thing that had to be beaten. I can remember how I felt when I looked at it. It was the symbol of my humiliation, the icon of my weakness, staring me in the face.

I knew that I couldn't avoid it, that I had to meet it again, but I also knew that I wasn't any stronger than the year before. I stood there watching, and I didn't laugh at any of the young boys who registered as wimps—I felt sorry for them. I knew it would soon be my turn and I didn't know what I was going to say or do. It was there and it had to be conquered.

As I was standing there, I noticed that my father was standing behind me. My dad is a very big man. He played football and lifted weights and grew up on a farm, and if he's anything, he's strong. The man said, "So, son, are you going to try again?" I said, "Yes, I am, only my dad is going to swing the sledgehammer for me."

I gave them the money and said, "Dad, it's your turn. You go show him what we Macks are made of." My dad went over and picked up that sledgehammer, and it was like a toy hammer to him, he was so strong. He took that sledgehammer and swung it over his head and banged it down. I watched that little silver thing shoot straight to the top. It rang the bell and the entire place stopped and looked because the noise was so loud. I said, "That's what Macks are made of, you see! We're he-men!"

This Lent, we're looking at the icon of our weakness, which is our cold, stony hearts. I can't break it, you can't break it. But there is One in our midst today who has the hammer that can break any heart. What we have to do is to go to Him and say, "If You can, will You do for me what I cannot do for myself?"

There was a third year the carnival came to town. We went back and I was so excited because my dad was going to impress every-body again. I was going to walk around and say, "See what we Macks are made of!" My dad was standing behind me and the man said, "Are you going to do it?" I said, "You bet I am. Go ahead, Dad." This year my father said, "No, son, I'm not going to do it for you this year."

I looked at him with absolute terror and said, "Dad, I'm not any stronger than I was two years ago. You cannot do this to me, please! I've been laughed at enough." He said, "Oh, son, you're not going to do it by yourself. We're going to swing the hammer to-gether." We walked over and I picked up the hammer, and it was just as heavy and I was just as weak.

My dad reached over and lifted the hammer and all of a sudden it was a lot lighter. He held it over my head and said, "Okay, on the count of three, we're going to let go. One, two, three!" and together we swung that hammer. That little silver thing went straight up again, and there was a loud ding at the top. I looked at my dad and said, "We did it! That's what we're made of, right?"

It's the third year that is Great Lent. Sometimes God swings the hammer all by Himself—thank God He does. Sometimes He just comes and breaks our hearts open. But most of the time God says, "Let's do it together." That's why Jesus at the end looked at His disciples and said, "Okay, I helped you this time. I covered you this time, I cast the demon out, but don't think I'm going to do that every time, because this kind can come out only by *prayer and fast-ing*. You wield that little toy hammer, and you beat your hard heart as hard as you can, and I promise that I will use My sledgehammer at the same time and together we will break open your heart and change you. Together we will drive away Satan and all his demons. Together we will come to the eternal Kingdom and dwell together there."

This kind comes out only by prayer and fasting. Don't despair of the little work you can do. Don't be proud of the little work you do, either. We can err on either side. We can be proud and say, "Look at what I'm doing." And God says, "I'm not going to help you, then," and we accomplish nothing. Or we can despair of the little that we're doing and not ask God for His help, and we accomplish nothing.

But in humility and in boldness we can take our little hammer and say, "God, You have to help me. You have to do this with me." If we ask in humility and faith, God will help us. St. Paul says, "Work out your own salvation with fear and trembling." Swing that little hammer, "for it is God who works in you both to will and to do for His good pleasure" (Phil. 2:12, 13).

chapter 25

The Dangers of Pride

Fifth Sunday of Lent, St. Mary of Egypt
Mark 10:32–45

Now they were on the road, going up to Jerusalem, and Jesus was going before them; and they were amazed. And as they followed they were afraid. Then He took the twelve aside again and began to tell them the things that would happen to Him: "Behold, we are going up to Jerusalem, and the Son of Man will be betrayed to the chief priests and to the scribes; and they will condemn Him to death and deliver Him to the Gentiles; and they will mock Him, and scourge Him, and spit on Him, and kill Him. And the third day He will rise again."

Then James and John, the sons of Zebedee, came to Him, saying, "Teacher, we want You to do for us whatever we ask." And He said to them, "What do you want Me to do for you?" They said to Him, "Grant us that we may sit, one on Your right hand and the other on Your left, in Your glory." But Jesus said to them, "You do not know what you ask. Are you able to drink the cup that I drink, and be baptized with the baptism that I am baptized with?" They said to Him, "We are able." So Jesus said to them, "You will indeed drink the cup that I drink, and with the baptism I am baptized with you will be baptized; but to sit on My right hand and on My left is not Mine to give, but it is for those for whom it is prepared."

And when the ten heard it, they began to be greatly displeased with James and John. But Jesus called them to Himself and said to them, "You know that those who are considered rulers over the Gentiles lord it over them, and their great ones exercise authority over them. Yet it shall not be so among you;

but whoever desires to become great among you shall be your servant. And whoever of you desires to be first shall be slave of all. For even the Son of Man did not come to be served, but to serve, and to give His life a ransom for many."

There is a story within our tradition that sets the stage for an understanding of this Gospel reading. It is found in the contemporary lives of the holy ascetics of Mt. Athos. There was a monk on Mt. Athos who was thought to be very holy. Everyone was speaking of this monk, and word had traveled throughout the entire community that this indeed was a very holy man—if not a saint, he was a saint in the making.

The word came to a hermit on top of the mountain who was truly holy that this holy elder was living down in the valley. He decided that he would go down and visit him, and they would share spiritual comfort and consolation. So he gathered his belongings and began the long, arduous walk from the top of the mountain down to the valley. He was filled with great joy, because it is a joy to meet and share words with a saint.

As he came close to the hut of the man who was reported to be a great saint, this holy man felt within him some disturbance. He began to question whether the rumors were true, whether this man he was going to see was indeed a holy man. So he stopped on the way and questioned a monk who was passing by, saying, "Tell me about the way of life of this holy man that I am going to see."

The monk said to him, "Father, he is so holy that we know he makes three thousand prostrations a day. He says a very lengthy prayer rule. He is very holy, Father, and you are in for a blessing." The man who was truly holy thought to himself, "If he makes three thousand prostrations a day, how do people know?"

He continued to walk, and as he approached the little hut in which the man who was reported to be a saint lived, he noticed that there was a crack in the door. He thought that was very strange, because most people do not have cracks in their doors. It was a fairly wide crack, maybe an inch and a half or two, and he noticed as he walked up the path leading to the hut that this crack was right in the line of vision of anyone walking up the path. He thought that was even more strange, almost as if the crack had been put there on purpose.

As he got closer, he realized that he could see right into the hut and through to the icon corner. As he stood looking through the crack, he saw the man who was reported to be a saint come over and position himself right in front of the icon corner, so that you could plainly see him from the path. Then he began to make his prostrations with a lot of noise.

The man who was indeed holy went up and opened the door. He said the usual monastic greeting. Then he spoke to the man who lived there. "You have been deceived by the devil. I forbid you in the name of God to make these prostrations, and I place you under obedience, if you care for your soul, to seal the crack in the door and to make thirty prostrations a day in secret." With that he left.

The rumor went throughout the Holy Mountain that this man had offended a saint. But the saints knew that he had spoken the truth. This man who was reported to be a saint did as he was instructed. He sealed the crack in the door. Several months went by, and the holy man went back down to see the other monk. When he walked in, the man met him with tears and said, "Father, I am an awful person. My life has come unglued. Father, I cannot make even thirty prostrations in secret."

The story has been told throughout the Holy Mountain to anyone who would aspire to the spiritual life. Be very careful, for your ego can hide behind pious acts. You can do holy things to feed your ego, and those holy actions will do you no good.

Satan loves it. If you were to ask Satan, "What is your perfect picture of a man whom you have consigned to hell?" I think that Satan would not respond by saying, "The perfect picture is the man who is living in debauchery and sin." Satan knows that the sinful man may come to realize the depravity of his way, and like the thief on the cross, he can go to heaven even if he repents on his deathbed.

Satan would say that the perfect victim, so far as he is concerned, is the man who has piety—enough piety so that he thinks he is holy, but who does all of his pious acts not for God, but so that he might feel good about himself, so that he might receive the praise of men. Satan would say that is the perfect catch, because that man thinks he is holy, so he does not think to repent. He thinks that everything he is doing will earn him the Kingdom, but it is doing no good because the root of his spiritual problem is his pride. Even his holy actions are feeding his pride.

If you understand that point, then you understand today's Gospel. Jesus sits with His disciples and says, "I have something very difficult to tell you, something which gives Me pain to speak of, and I know that it will give you pain. The Son of Man is going to Jerusalem and He will be condemned and beaten and crucified, and He will die at the hands of the Jews and the Roman authorities."

Then we read in the very next verse, "James and John came to Him secretly and said, 'Master, when you reign in Your kingdom, can we have spot number one and spot number two?'" Where were they when Jesus said, "I'm going to be crucified"? They didn't hear that. All they were concerned about was their pride and their ego.

Jesus said to them, "You cannot be number one and number two unless you are willing to die, unless you are willing to receive the baptism and drink from the cup that I drink of." In their great impulsiveness, they said, "Lord, we will drink it! We will drink it to the very dregs." Our Lord says, "You do not understand what you have just said. You do not understand that to reign with Me you must first suffer with Me, that before I can exalt you I must humble you. Before you can sit with Me in glory, your ego must be destroyed."

Then He says those words of mystery: "You indeed will drink the cup, you indeed will receive the baptism, but to sit on My right hand and on My left is not Mine to give. That is a mystery, and I do not reveal to you the fruits of your labors, lest you labor for the fruits—lest the labor itself feed your ego with visions of what you will be after you have consumed the chalice and received the baptism."

Jesus does not say this only to James and John; He says this to you and me. For everyone who would ascend to heaven must drink the cup that our Lord drank, and everyone who would reign with Christ must receive the baptism: the baptism of fire, of suffering, of death to self.

When the other ten heard through the rumor mill that James and John had been trying to sneak in and get ahead of them, they were indignant. Like children who are mad that someone else gets a bigger piece of the cake, they were angry that James and John had asked for honor before they themselves asked. Jesus calls them to Him and says, "You have it all wrong. If you think for a minute that following Me will feed your ego, if you think for a minute that becoming pious will make you loved by all men, and will give you authority and control over others, you are wrong.

"The way of the cross is not a way of feeding your ego; it is a way of destroying your ego. The way that I call you to walk is not a way that will make you feel good about yourself; it is a way that will make you hate yourself and your sin. The Son of Man did not come to be served, but to serve, and to give His life as a ransom for many."

We have come this week to the end of Lent. The Holy Church today reminds us to be very careful lest we do the duties and fulfill the disciplines so that we might feel good about ourselves and so that others might praise us. That is why in our tradition it is said that we must strive to hide all our spiritual labors. We don't have an Ash Wednesday, when we walk around with ashes on our head and proclaim to the world that we are fasting. We believe that is very dangerous.

We don't have sharing times in which we share the labors we have done for God, because we believe that is very dangerous. We do not speak to others of our spiritual accomplishments, but of our failures and our struggles. We do not complain when we are not recognized for what we have done. To tell others what we have accomplished can destroy all our spiritual labors, because in the last hour all the good that we have done can be perverted if we allow pride to enter into our souls.

The Fathers say that humility is the doorway that opens all the virtues. The Fathers also say that pride is the destruction of all the virtues. The great danger of the spiritual life is to be a Pharisee. You remember the Pharisees were not condemned because they did everything right; in fact, they were praised for that, even by God. The Pharisees were condemned because they took pride in what they had done, because they enjoyed having other people speak well of them. The Pharisees were condemned because they did the spiritual labors so that they might have positions of authority and tell other people how to live. They were condemned for their pride.

Today we celebrate St. Mary of Egypt, who is one of the holiest women ever to have walked on the face of the earth. We know that she is holy: she walked on water, and when she prayed she was lifted up. She labored for forty-seven years in the desert, and no one even knew she was there. No one ever said to her, "Thank you, Mary, you're doing a good job. Keep it up." Forty years of struggle and not one word of encouragement. Forty years in the desert, unknown to the world, but known to God and all the angels and all the saints.

She was revealed to the world not because of her need, but because of Zosima's need. She was only revealed to the world because people like Zosima thought they were perfect, because they had done everything. God had to show Zosima and the rest of us that perfection is not found in what we do.

St. Mary said upon her first meeting with Father Zosima, "Do not speak to anyone of what you have seen until after I have died." Why would she speak that word? Because she was afraid of pride. She who had labored for forty years in the desert was afraid that at the end she would be destroyed by pride. So she did not even give him her name until after she had died.

There is a story in our tradition from Russia of a holy priest who was traveling when he became deathly ill. He was a very holy man, extremely pious and devout. He was lying in an inn very sick, and they laid on the bed next to him another man who was equally sick. The second man was known to be as unholy as the priest was holy. He was a drunk, a womanizer, and everything that is unholy.

The priest smelled of incense from the church, and the drunk smelled of vodka from the tavern, and they both were dying. The priest turned his head and saw the drunk, and he began to thank

God: "Thank You for my pious parents, who raised me to love You and to know the Church. I thank You, God," and he listed all the things for which he was thankful. Then he said at the end, "I thank You, God, that I will not die like this unholy drunk."

As the holy man was saying his prayers, the drunk looked at him and said, "God, forgive me." He began to weep for his sins. As they were both about to die, a fool for Christ, a saint, walked in. He was sure that the soul of the drunk would be captured by the demons and taken off to hell, and the soul of the righteous priest would arise with the angels to heaven. He said to his disciple, "Look, now you will learn the lesson of life and see that all your labors will be rewarded."

The two men died, and God opened the eyes of the fool for Christ and of his disciple. They saw the angels and the demons coming down. The fool for Christ said to his disciple, "See, watch! Everything that I have taught you will be manifest here." The demons came, and they took the soul of the priest. The angels came, and they took the soul of the drunk.

The disciple turned to the fool for Christ in disbelief. He said, "How does this confirm everything that you have taught me?" The fool for Christ said, "God opposes the proud, but gives grace to the humble."

As we come to the end of Lent, be very careful. Do not let pride destroy what you have struggled to do with God's help this Lent. Do not let Satan steal these labors from you. Embrace humility. Repent more. Hide your labors from the eyes of others more, so that in humility we might be counted worthy to see the Passion of Christ and to worship His Holy Resurrection.

chapter 26

The Simplicity of Obedience

Sunday of the Paralytic

John 5:1–15

After this there was a feast of the Jews, and Jesus went up to Jerusalem. Now there is in Jerusalem by the Sheep Gate a pool, which is called in Hebrew, Bethesda, having five porches. In these lay a great multitude of sick people, blind, lame, paralyzed, waiting for the moving of the water. For an angel went down at a certain time into the pool and stirred up the water; then whoever stepped in first, after the stirring of the water, was made well of whatever disease he had.

Now a certain man was there who had an infirmity thirty-eight years. When Jesus saw him lying there, and knew that he already had been in that condition a long time, He said to him, "Do you want to be made well?" The sick man answered Him, "Sir, I have no man to put me into the pool when the water is stirred up; but while I am coming, another steps down before me." Jesus said to him, "Rise, take up your bed and walk."

And immediately the man was made well, took up his bed, and walked. And that day was the Sabbath. The Jews therefore said to him who was cured, "It is the Sabbath; it is not lawful for you to carry your bed." He answered them, "He who made me well said to me, 'Take up your bed and walk.'" Then they asked him, "Who is the Man who said to you, 'Take up your bed and walk'?" But the one who was healed did not know who it was, for Jesus had withdrawn, a multitude being in that place. Afterward Jesus found him in the temple, and said to him, "See, you have been made well. Sin no more, lest a worse

*thing come upon you." The man departed and told the Jews
that it was Jesus who had made him well.*

I wish I had been there to see this miracle. Can you imagine
what it would be like to be flat on a bed for thirty-eight years, watching all those around you walking to and fro, all alone, with no one
even to come and move you into the pool so that you could be
healed—and now, you can walk. Then as soon as you begin to walk,
someone tells you to stop walking.

I think I would have said in response, "You don't understand! I
haven't walked for thirty-eight years. This bed has carried me. I
have been stuck in this bed for this long time, and finally I can
walk, and I'm carrying this bed—don't tell me to stop, because I
intend to walk for the next thirty-eight years." I would have made a
defense.

Or perhaps I would have been intimidated by the religious authorities and the legal experts. Perhaps I would have dropped the
bed, because they didn't tell me not to walk, they just told me not to
carry the bed and walk. What difference does it make if I carry the
bed? I'm not going to need this bed anyway. If I had been on a bed
for thirty-eight years, I would have taken it and burned it, and rejoiced in the flames as they went up. I would have vowed never to
lie down again for the rest of my life.

But this man says something that we need to hear today. They
come and say, "Hey, stop! You're not allowed to carry your bed on
the Sabbath. Put it down! You're breaking the law." The man simply
says this: "I don't know anything. I'm a very simple man. I don't
know law—whether I'm allowed to carry the bed or not. I don't
know whether I walked a hundred yards with my bed or not. I only
know one thing: the man who made me well said to carry this bed,
and I am going to do what he said."

They said, "Who told you to do this? Who healed you?" And
the man said, "I don't have a clue. I told you already, I don't know
anything. I've been on a bed for the last thirty-eight years. The whole
world has passed me by. All I know is I used to lie on the bed, now
I can walk, he said carry the bed, and I'm doing it."

Most of us don't know this simplicity of obedience. We are far too sophisticated. We want to know why. It is not enough for the Church to tell us to do something. We have a long list of questions and we want every single question answered before we'll do what we're told. We want to understand before we obey.

That's very foolish, because there are many things we sinful people cannot understand. What's wrong with asking questions and insisting that we understand before we obey? By the time it has been explained to us, we no longer do it out of obedience; we do it because it is good for us. The Church tells us to fast, so we want to know all the reasons to fast. Then in our pride we can make the decision to fast because we know that it is good for us.

And in a very strange way, we then lose the reward of obedience. Not that it's always wrong to understand: the man who was healed did try to find out who it was that had healed him. But he didn't require all the information before he obeyed. He obeyed, and then he came to understand the wisdom of the command.

There are many things we cannot understand until we do them. But when in our humility we recognize that we don't know everything, and that there might possibly be a few people who have lived on this earth who know more than we do, and we decide to do what we're told—after we have begun to do it, we say, "Wow! This is a wonderful thing to do! This has helped me so much, I can't believe how good this has been for me." We never would have understood it, unless we had obeyed.

As we look at our tradition, there are many times when people are told to do things that are very silly. One example is the story of St. John the Dwarf, who became a monk and went to his spiritual father for counsel. His spiritual father gave him a dead stick and said, "Here, I want you to walk three miles into the desert and plant it."

Now if I had been told to take a stick and plant it in the desert three miles away, I think I would have asked a few questions. I think I would have insisted that my spiritual father undergo a psychological test to determine his sanity, before I obeyed. St. John the Dwarf took the stick and said, "With your blessing, Father," and he walked three miles into the desert and planted that stick. He walked back and said to his spiritual father, "I've done it." His father replied, "Very good. Now tomorrow morning I want you to take a bucket of water, walk three miles out into the desert, and water that stick that you just planted."

If I had gone out to plant the stick, I know I would have argued with him when he told me to go water the stick. I would have said, "Father, this is stupid. It's hot out there in the desert. I came here to pray and to learn how to be a monk, and you're sending me out into the desert to water a dead stick." I would have bargained with him: "Can I water every other day? How about once a week? I have things to do, I have responsibilities, I have a lot of things to take care of. That's a lot of time. Do you know how long it takes me to walk three miles into the desert, water the stick, and walk three miles back? And I have to take two buckets because half the water evaporates by the time I get there."

St. John the Dwarf said, "With your blessing, Father." He walked out, watered the stick, and came back. He said, "I've done it, Father." And the father said, "Good, I want you to do it again tomorrow."

I think at that point I would have quit. I would have said, "I'm finding a new monastery where they do reasonable things, like pray, make prostrations. Watering a dead stick in the desert—this has got to be the craziest thing I've ever heard of."

Every day for three years, St. John the Dwarf walked out with a bucket of water and watered a dead stick. He never asked his spiritual father why. He never argued with him. He never said, "Do you think I've learned the lesson? It's been a year, now; I think I've got the point. Can I go water something else? This is getting boring to water a stick every day."

On the third anniversary of the planting of that stick, he went out to water, and you know what he found? He found that the stick had come alive, and there were leaves and fruit growing from that dead stick. Now, if his spiritual father had told him, "If you do this for three years, that stick will become alive," if I were St. John, I would have said, "Now I know that you are positively crazy. Dead sticks do not come to life in the middle of the desert." Even if the explanation had been given, it would have been rejected.

St. John was obedient: he did what he was told without grumbling or complaining. Even if I had been holy enough to go out and water that stick, I think by the fourth day I would have begun to complain the whole way out and the whole way back. I think I would have been jealous of all the other men in the monastery who didn't have to go out and water a stick, and I would have wondered the whole way, "Why is he picking on me? What have I done that makes me the waterer of the dead stick in the desert? On my tombstone it will say, 'He who watered a dead stick.'"

St. John obeyed without grumbling or complaining. His obedience brought forth the miracle. New life sprang forth in the desert.

There's a lesson here for us. We are all very rebellious people. Just let somebody tell us to do something we don't want to do. We fight and complain and grumble; we become bitter. And sometimes we just disobey: "Forget it, I don't care what the bishop says, I'm going to do my own thing. I don't care what my father confessor says, I'm going to do my own thing. I don't care what my father and mother say, I'm going to do my own thing."

The paralytic said, "I don't know, I don't understand. All I know is that the man who made me well said do it, and I'm going to obey." May God grant us grace to learn obedience and to see its fruits. May God grant us the grace to be obedient children to our father confessor.

It is a very difficult thing to be a father confessor today. Many times father confessors don't say anything, because they know it will not be received. They're quiet, even though they know the medicine that will heal the soul, because they know that there is no spirit of obedience. And so many people are not healed because they are not obedient. The spiritual fathers and the father confessors weep over the obstinate hearts of their children. They weep over children who fight back and argue, instead of saying, "With your blessing."

May this example of the paralytic break our cold, obstinate hearts. May we face what is being said, and in honesty admit that we are rebellious. And may we come to ourselves and be willing to obey, so that we will live to see the miracles of obedience—the flowering of our cold hearts and the bearing of the fruit of the Spirit in our lives.

chapter 27

Divine Power

Pentecost Sunday
John 7:37 52, 8:12
On the last day, that great day of the feast, Jesus stood and cried out, saying, "If anyone thirsts, let him come to Me and drink. He who believes in Me, as the Scripture has said, out of his heart will flow rivers of living water." But this He spoke concerning the Spirit, whom those believing in Him would receive; for the Holy Spirit was not yet given, because Jesus was not yet glorified.
. . . Then Jesus spoke to them again, saying, "I am the light of the world. He who follows Me shall not walk in darkness, but have the light of life."

A number of years ago, I bought a house. I was very excited about the house because it had a detached double garage. The garage had lights and nice shelves, and electrical outlets that were appropriately placed. I could set up a little workshop in that garage.

When we bought the house, I excitedly moved my things in. I even asked my father-in-law if he would give me a table saw. I was so excited that I had a table saw and a drill and everything I needed. I was going to become a woodworker and teach my boys how to work with wood. It was going to be wonderful.

So once we had moved in, I ran out to the garage and plugged in the table saw. I got out a piece of wood, and I was ready to cut it in half. I reached down and turned on the saw—and there was nothing.

I thought to myself, "What a father-in-law! He buys me a broken machine." So I said, "Forget it, I'm not going to use his

155

machine, I'm going to use my jigsaw, because I know it works." I plugged in my jigsaw and got out the piece of wood. I turned it on—and nothing. By now I was getting a bit frustrated and it was getting dark. I thought, "I'd better turn on the lights." I hit the light switch—and there was nothing.

I went inside completely disgusted, not knowing what was wrong. The next day I called in an electrician, who came out to look at the wiring. He came into the garage and looked around and said, "There's nothing wrong here. Let's go outside and check on the wiring that comes into the garage."

We went out the side door and I heard him say, "Ah, here's the problem. There's no electricity run to the garage. It's all set up on the inside, perfectly, but there's no wire run from the house to the garage." Then he looked at me and said, "You've been had. They didn't want to spend the money to run the electrical wiring to the garage, but they knew that they could sell the house more easily if they made it look like there was electricity in the garage." So it looked perfect: all set up, but there was no power. And because there was no power, nothing worked.

If you understand that illustration, then you understand the significance of the Feast of Pentecost. The Church is like my garage. We can do what the couple did who lived in my house before I bought it, and set the Church up to look perfect. We can have the right vestments, the right prayers, the right people—we can have everything completely correct. But if there is no power, if there is no Holy Spirit, then nothing works. And we cannot run the wire from heaven to us. God has to run it.

Today we celebrate not the birthday of the Church, because the Church existed from before time, but rather the giving of the Holy Spirit to the Church. On the Day of Pentecost, the Church was empowered by the presence of God Himself.

One of the most striking aspects of the Old Testament is how the people of God could not stay faithful to Him. God set up a wonderful church in the Old Testament, with the proper rituals, the proper buildings, the proper leaders, but throughout the entire Old Testament the people of God are always turning away from

God to false idols. He has to send His prophets to call them back, and then they kill the prophets.

Even the holiest people in the Old Testament—David the King, Abraham—none of them could sustain the faith of the one true God. David committed adultery with Bathsheba. Abraham had difficulty believing God's promise, and worked in all kinds of deceptive and conniving ways in order to fulfill it.

What was missing? Today's Gospel explains it: "For the Holy Spirit was not yet given." It is an amazing thing that for the two thousand years before Christ, the people of God could not keep the faith. But in the two thousand years after Christ, the people of God have kept the faith, and we have the faith today.

What is the difference? Is it that there were better people who lived after Christ than before Christ? We know that the answer is no. The difference is that the Holy Spirit was given to the Church. The Holy Spirit is the power of the Church, and He gives us the power to live holy lives. That's why we pray, "O Heavenly King, O Comforter, the Spirit of truth, who are in all places and fill all things, the treasury of good things and the giver of life, come and *abide* in us, cleanse us from every stain, and save our souls, O Good One."

Nearly every prayer service begins with that invocation to the Holy Spirit. Without the Holy Spirit, without His energizing power and His sanctifying presence, everything we do is worthless and empty. This is why St. Seraphim says that the goal of the Christian life is the acquisition of the Holy Spirit. What a difference it makes when our actions are fueled, not by our own strength, or our own thought, decisions, or plans, but by the thoughts and plans of God the Holy Spirit.

Many of us think too much and pray too little. When a problem comes, we sit down and try to figure it all out rationally. We make decisions on the basis of what we have thought. We say, "This is the right thing to do," and we attempt it and it fails and we wonder, "What went wrong?" We thought too much and prayed too little, because we never stopped to ask God if what we had decided to do was His plan.

My observation of God's dealing with us is that God very often picks the most unreasonable and irrational way to do things. God's plan is very often one that doesn't make sense to us.

Look at Gideon: He finally gathered his major army with thousands and thousands of men, and God said, "There are too many. You need to get rid of some." Gideon said, "If anyone is afraid, go home." Half of them left and Gideon said, "Well, I think I can still do it with this group," and God said, "There's still too many. You have to get rid of them, Gideon. How do you expect to win a battle if you have a lot of soldiers?"

Gideon said, "How can you win any other way?" But God said, "My plan is not your plan. Gideon, get rid of most of them. Keep three hundred and you'll defeat the tens of thousands of Midianites, because I will be with you." And of course it worked (cf. Judges 7).

Today we celebrate the giving of God the Holy Spirit to the Church, and to us as members of the Church. We have the Holy Spirit so long as we remain united in a living way to the Church, and when we fall away from the Church we lose the Holy Spirit and His presence in our hearts. We celebrate and give thanks to God that we don't have to reason our way out of every situation, that we don't have to find our own strength to do things.

How often have people said to me, "I can't win this battle against sin! I can't beat my passions. I'm overwhelmed!" And I say, "Thank God you don't have to win the battle against sin by yourself, because the battle against sin is not won by you. It is won by God." God is the victor, insofar as we give ourselves over to Him, insofar as we say to Him, "Your agenda is my agenda, whatever that agenda may be. Your thoughts are my thoughts. Your ways are my ways," and as we wait in patience upon God, as the disciples waited in that holy upper room.

Jesus said, "You wait, and the power of the Holy Spirit will come upon you" (cf. Acts 1:5, 8). How long did they wait for the Spirit to come? Ten days. Some of us can't wait ten minutes. We ask God and we say, "Okay, let's go." Nothing comes and we say, "I guess God isn't going to help—I'm going to have to do this one by myself."

We attempt to do it by ourselves, and we fall flat on our faces.

We think when we begin to fall that if we just exert more energy, we'll be able to do it. We muster all our energy and what happens is that we fall faster and we're more tired when we hit.

We have to learn to wait for God. We have to learn to ask for God's blessing and God's presence. That's why in our tradition we're told, "Don't do anything without a blessing," because it teaches us to wait, to remember that we do not do things in our own strength. We do them in the strength of God Almighty.

The Holy Spirit is not conjured up by our activity. He's not impressed with our energy and our strength. The Holy Spirit is brought into our midst by fervent prayer, by an acknowledgment of our own weakness. When we come to the end of ourselves and we have nothing left and we say, "Come, Holy Spirit, come," then He comes. And He does in our hearts and in our community and in the lives of others that which we cannot do by ourselves.

That is the gift. He is the gift we celebrate today. If we come to Him, God will do for us what we cannot do for ourselves. He will give us victory over sin. He will give us victory over our passions. He will become for us light and life. He will come and abide in us, cleanse us from every stain, and save our souls.

chapter 28

The Church of the Saints

Sunday of All Saints
Matthew 10:32, 33, 37, 38; 19:27–30

"Therefore whoever confesses Me before men, him I will also confess before My Father who is in heaven. But whoever denies Me before men, him I will also deny before My Father who is in heaven. . . . He who loves father or mother more than Me is not worthy of Me. And he who loves son or daughter more than Me is not worthy of Me. And he who does not take his cross and follow after Me is not worthy of Me."

. . . Then Peter answered and said to Him, "See, we have left all and followed You. Therefore what shall we have?" So Jesus said to them, "Assuredly I say to you, that in the regeneration, when the Son of Man sits on the throne of His glory, you who have followed Me will also sit on twelve thrones, judging the twelve tribes of Israel. And everyone who has left houses or brothers or sisters or father or mother or wife or children or lands, for My name's sake, shall receive a hundredfold, and inherit eternal life. But many who are first will be last, and the last first."

This Sunday is everyone's name day, because on this day we celebrate all the saints who have lived and labored and prayed from the beginning of time until now. The Exapostilarion for this day says: "As a duty let us crown with songs of praise the Forerunner, with the Apostles, Prophets, Martyrs, Bishops, righteous ones, with all the God-fearing and the myriads of angels, beseeching, through their petitions, that we may attain by their glory, glory from the presence of Christ the Savior."

The list of saints whom the Church honors is very large, but we know it is not complete, for there are many saints who have lived who are unknown to us. God chooses to reveal saints to the world at certain times because their lives have specific meaning for us in our struggles. The saints can sometimes remain hidden for long periods before God reveals them to us.

So this is a great and wondrous feast day, a feast day of great joy and celebration. Metropolitan Hierotheos of Vlachos says that the proof of any church is not to be found in the rational argumentation it offers in defense of its doctrine, because rational arguments can be made for anything. The proof of the Church is certainly not to be found in the money she has amassed, or in the buildings she has built, or in her influence in the world. Rather, the proof of the Orthodox Church is in her saints. The saints prove that this is the place where God the Holy Spirit dwells.

Jesus said in John 15:4–6: "Abide in Me, and I in you. As the branch cannot bear fruit of itself, unless it abides in the vine, neither can you, unless you abide in Me. I am the vine, you are the branches. He who abides in Me, and I in him, bears much fruit; for without Me you can do nothing. If anyone does not abide in Me, he is cast out as a branch and is withered; and they gather them and throw them into the fire, and they are burned."

We ask, "What fruit will manifest that we are connected to the life of God?" In Galatians 5:22, 23, St. Paul says that the fruit of the Spirit is love, joy, peace, longsuffering, kindness, goodness, faithfulness, gentleness, self-control.

How do we know that this Church is connected to the very life of God? How do we know that this is where God the Holy Spirit dwells, and that if we want to be connected to the energy of God the Holy Spirit we must be connected to the Church? Because where the Spirit lives, there are produced men and women who are love, who are joy, who are peace, who are patience, who are longsuffering, who are kindness, who are goodness, who are faithfulness, who are gentleness, who are self-control.

He produces people who *are* these things, not people who have these things episodically. You and I have them episodically. Every now and then we have love—it comes and it goes. Every now and then—rarely for those of us who have children—we have patience. Every now and then we have joy, or peace, or longsuffering, or kindness.

The saints, the holy ones, do not *have* love—they *are* love. They do not have joy, they are joy. They do not have peace, they are peace. The story is told of one father, recently reposed, who was living in the northern woods of California in a little cell. You would go to see him with a list of questions you had to have answered. You would come into his cell, and you would sit and talk with him a bit. Then you would leave and realize that you hadn't asked any of the questions. When you were in his presence you didn't need to ask questions, because there was a peace of God that flooded your soul and made the questions unimportant. You would leave knowing that you had come up against peace in the flesh. The saints are peace.

The saints are patience. They are longsuffering. Look at the martyrs and the stories of what they endured. We say, "How could they have endured that? There's no way I could have endured." St. Gregory the Enlightener of Armenia was in a pit for fourteen years, living with snakes, being fed every couple of weeks with bread that was dropped down by a friend. How could he endure that kind of suffering? Because he was a saint and he was longsuffering in the flesh.

The saints are kindness, because they are indwelt with the Holy Spirit. They themselves become the fruit of the Holy Spirit. How do we know that this is the Church, and that God dwells here? The answer is found in the saints. It was by clinging to the Church that the saints found God.

One of my favorite lines from the Psalms says, "The mountain of God is a butter mountain, a curdled mountain is the mountain of the Lord. Why suppose you that there be other curdled mountains?" (Ps. 68:15, 16, LXX). Now what does that mean? It sounds very strange, this mountain of butter and curds—except when you've been fasting for a while. What is meant is that the mountain of the Lord is rich in grace.

The mountain of the Lord is Mount Zion, which is the Church. The Church is full of grace and full of the Holy Spirit, and she feeds us. Then the psalmist says, "Why suppose you that there are other curdled mountains?" Why do you worry about whether you can find grace anywhere else? Grace is here in abundance. Why do you worry about whether there are other ways to heaven? This is the way to heaven.

What we need to do is to center our attention and our love on the Church of God, and stop looking for easier, less arduous ways, or ways that are more fun, or ways that are new and exciting. This is a butter mountain, this is a mountain of curds, this is the habitation of God the Holy Spirit.

How do we know? We know because this is the Church that has produced the saints. Saints in abundance have lived in this Church. In our own times we have St. John of San Francisco, who all the world—Protestant, Roman Catholic, and Orthodox—agreed was the holiest man alive. He dwelt in this Church. We can think back a few years to St. Raphael. He dwelt in this Church. St. Herman of Alaska and St. Seraphim of Sarov, men that the entire world said were holy, grace-bearing men, lived in this Church.

We think back in time before then, to the great Fathers of the Church: St. John Chrysostom, St. Gregory the Theologian, St. Basil the Great. They lived in this Church. The great defenders of the faith—St. Athanasius, St. Gregory of Nyssa—lived in this Church. The holy martyrs—St. Barbara, St. Anastasia, St. Photini, St. Katherine—lived in this Church. Think back to the days of the Apostles: St. John the Apostle and Evangelist, St. Paul, St. Peter, St. Nathaniel, St. Andrew the First-Called, St. Timothy. They all dwelt in this Church.

This is the Church of the saints. This is where we know God the Holy Spirit dwells, because "by their fruits you will know them" (Matt. 7:20). "The mountain of God is a butter mountain, it is a mountain of curds. Why suppose you that there be other butter mountains?"

chapter 29

God Will Provide

Third Sunday after Pentecost
Matthew 6:25–33

"Therefore I say to you, do not worry about your life, what you will eat or what you will drink; nor about your body, what you will put on. Is not life more than food and the body more than clothing? Look at the birds of the air, for they neither sow nor reap nor gather into barns; yet your heavenly Father feeds them. Are you not of more value than they? Which of you by worrying can add one cubit to his stature? So why do you worry about clothing? Consider the lilies of the field, how they grow: they neither toil nor spin; and yet I say to you that even Solomon in all his glory was not arrayed like one of these.

"Now if God so clothes the grass of the field, which today is, and tomorrow is thrown into the oven, will He not much more clothe you, O you of little faith? Therefore do not worry, saying, 'What shall we eat?' or 'What shall we drink?' or 'What shall we wear?' For after all these things the Gentiles seek. For your heavenly Father knows that you need all these things. But seek first the kingdom of God and His righteousness, and all these things shall be added to you."

I once heard the story of a man who worried about everything. He worried constantly about having enough money to pay his bills each month, about the food he was going to eat. He worried about his health, about his children, about his wife. He worried about whether or not he would have his job the next day. He worried about everything.

He was known throughout the town as one who was consumed

by anxiety. The wrinkles caused by worry had formed on his face. People got used to the frown, the look of intensity and anxiety, that was always on his face.

One day, as he was walking down the street, everyone in the town was amazed because the look of worry was gone. The brow that had always been furrowed was now smooth. The mouth that had been perpetually tense was now smiling. The rumor went out that the man was no longer worrying. Everyone gathered to see this wondrous event. Finally someone had the courage to go up to him and say, "What happened? Why are you no longer consumed by worry?"

The man smiled and said, "Let me tell you what happened to me yesterday. I met a man who said if I paid him a thousand dollars a week, he would do all my worrying for me. So I hired him in an instant, and he's now worrying for me, and I don't have to worry about a thing. I can be happy."

They looked at him in amazement and said, "How in the world are you going to pay him a thousand dollars a week?" He said, "I don't know, that's his worry."

Our Lord in today's Gospel says something very striking. We've heard this so many times that we gloss over it. We tend to take the words of Scripture and shave off the edges so that our lives can continue the same way. But we need to hear the exact words of Jesus in this passage, and we need to believe that Jesus means exactly what He says. He says, "Take no thought [KJV] for what you will eat or what you will wear or where you will live, for after all these things the Gentiles seek, but your Father knows what you need. Seek first the kingdom of God and His righteousness, and all these things will be added to you."

Now Jesus does not say, "Take a few thoughts about what you will eat and what you will drink and what you will wear and where you will live." He does not say, "You may spend ten percent of your time worrying about these things, and ninety percent of your time should be spent thinking about heavenly things." He does not say, "On Mondays you are allowed to be consumed with worries and thoughts."

Jesus says, "Take no thought, for after all these things the pagans and the Gentiles seek. But you are to be consumed with thoughts of the Kingdom. If you must worry, then worry about your soul. If you must plan for the future, then plan how you will live more holy tomorrow than you do today. Seek first the Kingdom of God and His righteousness."

Everybody says, "Aha, see, He says 'seek first,' so there has to be a 'seek second,' right?" That's not what Jesus means. He means, "Seek *only* the kingdom of God and His righteousness." If you seek God first, there is no second. It would be the equivalent of my saying to my wife, "You are first in my life, and this lady in Orlando is second, and a lady in California is third." She would rightly say to me, "No, I'm first and only, or I'm not in your life at all."

God says that to us. We don't seek first God and secondly our health, and thirdly our wealth, etc. We seek first God and His righteousness, and we take no thought for anything else. That's a very radical teaching. Does God really mean that we're not supposed to plan? Does God really mean that we're not supposed to think about what we eat and what we drink? That's what He says: "no thought."

And He holds up examples that are very extreme. He asks, "Why do you worry about how you look? Why do you take care for the clothes you wear and become obsessed with that? Look at the flowers of the field. God takes care of them, and they're more beautiful than you will ever be." No flower ever woke up on any morning and began to worry, "What will I wear today? What will I look like to all those people who walk by?" They don't even think about that. God takes care of them, and they are beautiful. He says, "Even Solomon in all his glory cannot be compared to one of these."

He says, "Consider the birds of the air." They don't hoard up, they don't have a bank account. They don't save gold bullion in the base of their nest for a rainy day. They just exist, they live. And yet, Jesus says, God provides for them and they have more than they need. "Seek first the kingdom of God and His righteousness, and all these things will be added to you."

Of course, this doesn't mean that we can sit at home and do nothing, and expect that there's going to be a knock on the door.

The swallows don't worry, but they do work. God expects us to work and to use the gifts that He has given to us. But He expects us to invest in the Kingdom of God and His righteousness. He expects us to be thinking throughout the day about how we can live for God more truly, to be concerned about the state of our souls, to be thinking of the Kingdom and of His righteousness.

When those satanic thoughts come and oppress you with worries about your financial future, or about your health, or how you're going to handle something that may come months or years from now, say to Satan, "That's not my worry, that's God's worry. I'm seeking first the Kingdom of God, and God has promised that He will take care of me. You go talk to God about that and see what He has to say."

Jesus goes on in the next verse to say, "Do not worry about tomorrow. Tomorrow will take care of itself. Sufficient unto each day is the trouble thereof." God wants us to live in the here and now, not in tomorrow. God wants us to deal with today and trust Him to take care of tomorrow.

How many times have you worried about something, spent countless hours preparing for it, only to find out that what you had worried about wasn't nearly as big a deal as you thought it was going to be? How many times have you come up against something that you have not prepared for at all, and wondered, how am I going to get through this? God gets you through it, and you look back in amazement that you survived, not only survived but flourished through something that you weren't prepared for.

Why is it that we can look back and see that God has done that for us in the past, but we can't look into the future and believe that God would do it again? Why is it that we think we can take better care of the future than God? It's very silly, because God knows the future, and if I invest in God today, God will reward me tomorrow, far better than I could reward myself.

The story of St. Philaret the Merciful illustrates this beautifully. St. Philaret was a wealthy man and an almsgiver, and through a series of events outside his control he went from wealth to poverty. His family lived in a little shack, and had only a little plot of ground and one cow—one cow with which to plow, one cow to give milk for them to drink.

St. Philaret was working in his fields one day when his neighbor's cow died. The neighbor began to weep about how he wouldn't be able to support his children. St. Philaret said, "Here, take my cow. I'll be fine without a cow."

He went home and his wife said, "Where's the cow?" St. Philaret said, "She's not mine anymore." The wife looked at St. Philaret and said, "You didn't, did you? How could you think of giving away our only cow? I wasn't happy when we were rich and you gave away everything, but now you're giving away everything when we're poor. How in the world will we survive?"

That's Satan's question: Whenever you do God's will, he says, "How are you going to make it?" Hear that question, and recognize that that's the voice of the evil one.

St. Philaret said, "God will provide." His wife said, "That's easy for you to say. You say that about everything." St. Philaret said, "You wait, God will provide."

Very shortly thereafter, the emperor sent emissaries throughout the countryside to find a wife for his son, and St. Philaret's granddaughter was chosen. He was exalted to a position of great power and wealth. He said to his wife, "See? God will provide." Seek first the Kingdom of God and His righteousness, and all of these things will be added to you.

There's another story about St. John of San Francisco. When St. John was in China, he saw many babies that were being left to die because they were unwanted. His heart was filled with compassion, and he never stopped to ask, "How can we take care of them?" He only asked, "What does God want me to do?" and left the "How can we pay for that?" to God, because he knew that was God's business.

He gathered up all these children—in time, over 3,500 orphans in the city of Shanghai. He gave them all the houses that were set aside for the bishops. All he asked was a little room, like a closet, upstairs in one of these houses.

One day he came home from the evening vigil and the woman who was in charge of the orphanage was shaking her finger at him, screaming before he even came in. She said, "How dare you do this? What right do you have to do this to these children, to give them hope, and then not to provide for them? We have no food and no money. How are we going to feed these hungry children in the morning?"

St. John looked at her and smiled. He said, "God will provide." She said, "You say that every time. That may work in church, but this is the real world, and there are real children with really hungry bellies. You tell them tomorrow that God will provide as they sit at the table with nothing to eat."

He gave her that look that I'm sure Jesus gave when He said, "O you of little faith"—that look that says, "When will they learn that they live in the fake world, and I live in the real world?" He said again, "God will provide." She knew that there was no point in talking to him, so she went back into the kitchen and stared at the empty shelves.

He climbed the steps and all of a sudden she heard a thud, then another. She went up the steps and stood by his door, and she knew that he was making prostrations. She muttered under her breath, "Oh sure, go pray now. There are hungry children. The least he could do is go out and start knocking on doors and asking for bread. But what does he do? He goes up in his room and begins to pray." It made her even more angry, and she couldn't sleep because all night long she heard *thud, thud*. St. John prostrated himself for six and a half hours straight.

As she got up in the morning she heard the thuds coming from his room and thought, "Well, I hope he kills himself. Then he'll learn what the real world is like." She came down the steps and there was a knock on the door. She opened the door, and there was a man with his hat in his hands saying, "Excuse me, ma'am. I was on my way to market with a truck full of bread, and my truck just broke down. I have nothing to do with this bread, and I can't wait because it will go bad in the heat. Can I give you this truckload of bread, and can you find something to do with it?"

Just then St. John came down the steps to leave for the morning service. He looked at her and said, "God will provide."

You say, "Why don't those things happen to me?" It's probably because you don't prostrate through the night. It's probably because you're worried and obsessed with taking care of yourself. It's probably because you don't believe that the real world is one in which God provides for His people.

God will provide. Seek first the Kingdom of God and His righteousness, and all these things will be added to you. That is a promise of God. You are not important enough for God to risk His reputation on. He has never lied to a human being yet, and He's not going to start with you. God will keep His word. You can take God's word to the bank, because God's word is as good as gold. Seek first the Kingdom of God and His righteousness, and all these things will be added unto you.

chapter 30

You Are the Light of the World

Fourth Sunday after Pentecost
Matthew 5:14–19
"You are the light of the world. A city that is set on a hill cannot be hidden. Nor do they light a lamp and put it under a basket, but on a lampstand, and it gives light to all who are in the house. Let your light so shine before men, that they may see your good works and glorify your Father in heaven.

"Do not think that I came to destroy the Law or the Prophets. I did not come to destroy but to fulfill. For assuredly, I say to you, till heaven and earth pass away, one jot or one tittle will by no means pass from the law till all is fulfilled. Whoever therefore breaks one of the least of these commandments, and teaches men so, shall be called least in the kingdom of heaven; but whoever does and teaches them, he shall be called great in the kingdom of heaven."

This is a very important passage in the Gospels, one of those famous lines that has been repeated by many throughout history. But what exactly is Jesus saying when He says, "You are the light of the world"?

There are three questions we have to ask as we look at that verse. The first is reasonably simple to answer: What is the meaning of "the world"? We know that the world is this earth and all who live on it. Everything that exists on the earthly plane—all the governments, the institutions, the communities, the individuals—comprises and constitutes the world.

God is concerned for the world—not for a small portion of the world, but for the entire world and for every person who has lived or will live. God loves all men the same, and He loves us infinitely with that love that is His very nature, for as St. John says, "God is love" (1 John 4:8).

The second question is, what does Jesus mean by "light"? He goes on to say, "Let your light so shine before men that they may see your good works and glorify your Father who is in heaven." On a casual reading, we might come to the conclusion that the light we are to shine is our good works.

There are many who understand this simply to mean that you are the moral compass of the world. You are to live lives that are characterized by good works, and the good works are the light that will shine and show other people how to live. They will learn from you what is right and what is wrong.

Now that is true—that we are to live holy lives, that we are by the example of our lives to teach others how to live, that we Christians must not conform to the patterns of this world, but, as St. Paul says in Romans 12:2, "be transformed by the renewing of your mind, that you may prove what *is* that good and acceptable and perfect will of God." The New Testament has a great deal to say about the necessity of good works.

We know from Matthew 6 what those good works are: fasting, prayer, almsgiving. So we are to be people who fast, who pray, who give alms, who keep the law of God. "Whoever therefore breaks one of the least of these commandments, and teaches men so, shall be called least in the kingdom of heaven," says Jesus, "but whoever does and teaches them, he shall be called great in the kingdom of heaven." We are to examine everything we do and think and feel by the commandments of Christ. St. Paul says in 2 Corinthians 10:5 that we are to take every thought captive and make it obedient to Christ.

But I am convinced that even though this is true, this is not all that Jesus means when He says, "You are the light of the world." The light that we are to let shine upon the world is not the light of our good deeds. Rather, what He says is, "Let your light shine so that men who see that light may then ask how you got that light, and they may see your good works and thus they may glorify your

Father who is in heaven." The good works are important, but the good works are not the light.

What is the light? In John 8:12, Jesus says, "I am the light of the world." It's the exact same sentence as in Matthew 5—only now it's not, "You are the light of the world," but, "I am the light of the world." The light that we are to let shine is the light of Christ, because He is the light.

It is not our good works; there is no light in our good works. We have no source of light in ourselves. Jesus is the light of the world. And St. John says in John 1:4, "In Him was life, and the life was the light of men." We look to the Mount of Transfiguration, and there we see a revelation of who Jesus really is, as He shines with all His brilliance and all His glory. Even His clothes became bright and shining, and it was so glorious that the disciples fell down and could not look upon the light that came forth from His raiment and from His face (cf. Matt. 17:1–8).

We are reminded of Moses, who went up on the mountain and conversed with God. When he came down the people said, "Hide your face, we cannot stand to look upon it," because Moses was glowing with the light of God (cf. Ex. 34:29–35).

God is light, and in Him there is no darkness. Jesus is the light of the world. He says something amazing: "You are the light of the world. Just as I have shone forth the divine glory, so you shine forth that same glory to the world. And when I am no longer here, you will be My presence in the world. I will not leave this world, because you will be here, and just as I have shown the world my glory on the mountain, so you in the mountains and in the valleys and in your homes and at work are to shine forth the glory of Christ."

We should not spiritualize this by saying that somehow this is light that we can't see. The light of which Jesus speaks is *light*. We know that from the stories of the saints. Not too long ago, in the early part of this century, there was a hieromonk at Valaam Monastery who, every time he served Liturgy, would shine as Jesus did on the Mount of Transfiguration. He would become illumined and his face would be so bright that the priests who were serving with him asked him if he would cover his face, because the light that came forth from him was so bright that they could not stand it. So he would take the aer, and when he was finished shaking it during the reciting of the Creed, he would cover his face with it. He would serve Liturgy with the aer cloth over his face so that those who were there in the altar could abide his presence.

We're reminded of the holy Desert Father who said to his disciples, "Do you want to know what it means to be saved? Look at this." He held up his hand, and from his hand came rays of light. We're reminded of St. John in the sixth century who locked himself in his cell. He was in his cell for so many years that his disciples became concerned. When they opened the door of the cell a beam of light streaked out and went to heaven, because St. John had been consumed and had become the light of Christ.

You are the light of the world. You are the presence of Christ in the world. This world is filled with darkness. There is no light in this world. But Jesus says you are the source of light for mankind. This brings us to the question, who is the "you"?

If we look at ourselves, we know that we're not the "you." I don't shine with the light of Christ. I look in my life, and I see a lot of darkness. The "you" are the saints of God, those who have progressed through purification and illumination and have become filled with the light of Christ. They shine forth the light of Christ.

Have you ever noticed that in icons of the saints the light is coming from within the saint? That is what makes icons very different from paintings. In painting there is always an external source of light that produces shadows. But in icons, there are no shadows, because the light is not external. It is the saint who is the source of light, because that saint is the light of the world. Just as Jesus was the light of the world, that saint, being filled with God, in communion with Christ, is filled with the light of God, and the saint shines with the brilliance of the Father's glory. They are the lights of the world.

But we must come to a deeper meaning. It is true that there is no light in me, or very little, and that the saints are the light of the world. But I cannot leave it there, because there is no doubt that when Jesus says, "You are the light of the world," he is speaking to all of His disciples. He is telling them what they must become.

At that moment, none of the disciples was the light of the world. The disciples were not illumined and deified until Pentecost, when they received the outpouring of the Holy Spirit. So at that moment when Jesus said, "You are the light of the world," they were not shining, because they had not seen His glory. So Jesus is saying, "You must become the light of the world. That is what I have called you to be. Until you shine with My light, then you have not yet lived up to your calling."

There is so much more for us to do. You remember the story of the desert father and his hand of light? He did that because his disciples were all sitting around thinking that they had done pretty well in the spiritual life, that they had made it, that they were examples to the world because they kept vigil and kept the fasts and did everything right. The father got upset and said, "You think this is all there is? You think that this is what it means to follow Christ? Until you can do this, you have not yet begun to follow Christ." And he held up his hand and it shot out beams of light.

This is what we have been called to do. We have not been called to be like the world. We have not been called to be liked by the world. We have not been called to be as close to the world as we can be without crossing over the line and entering into sin.

God has called us to become pillars of light. God has called us to be purified of our passions and our sins, to be illumined with divine grace, to be deified by His indwelling, and to become the lights of the world. We all are called to be saints. That is why we are here. Unless we see that, we will not live up to the blessing that God has given us.

The saints are not the unusual ones. They're not a separate class that we look at in awe and say, "Oh, I could never be like that." The saints are like us. They were sinners like us, they were raised by parents who were sinners like us, they lived in a sinful world like us, they had passions like us, they had temptations like us. The evil one is no stronger today than he was when they lived.

But the saints lived up to the calling to become the lights of the world. They beckon to us, saying, "You can do better. You can try harder. Don't despair. You can beat that sin. I know, because I beat that sin before you. Don't think that your struggle is greater than mine; we struggle the same way, and if I struggled by the grace and power of God, you can too. If you think you're not worthy, then you're right, because I wasn't worthy. And if you think you're not capable, you're right, because I wasn't capable."

God's grace is greater than all our sin, because we don't have to generate that light. God is the light, and it is His light that shines through us. What we have to do is to rid ourselves of all the darkness, all the things that clutter up our souls and leave no room for God. We have to do those good works that show God we're serious, but the best we can do is not very good. It's not our good works that produce light—God produces light.

Ultimately, we have to want to be illumined. If you want to become the light of the world, God will make you the light of the world. He will do it in unusual ways; He will make your life very difficult at times. But if that's what you want, then that's what will happen. We have to say to God, "I want to be the light of the world, and I don't care what it costs. I don't care how arduous it is; I want to be what You want me to be. I want to shine with Your glory. I want to be filled with Your presence. I want to become what the saints already are. I want to be the light of the world."

chapter 31

Spiritual Warfare

Fifth Sunday after Pentecost
Matthew 8:28—9:1

*When He had come to the other side, to the country of the
Gergesenes, there met Him two demon-possessed men, coming
out of the tombs, exceedingly fierce, so that no one could pass
that way. And suddenly they cried out, saying, "What have we
to do with You, Jesus, You Son of God? Have You come here to
torment us before the time?"*

*Now a good way off from them there was a herd of many
swine feeding. So the demons begged Him, saying, "If You cast
us out, permit us to go away into the herd of swine." And He
said to them, "Go." So when they had come out, they went into
the herd of swine. And suddenly the whole herd of swine ran
violently down the steep place into the sea, and perished in the
water.*

*Then those who kept them fled; and they went away into
the city and told everything, including what had happened to
the demon-possessed men. And behold, the whole city came out
to meet Jesus. And when they saw Him, they begged Him to
depart from their region. So He got into a boat, crossed over,
and came to His own city.*

Let us think about what the demons in this Gospel story say
when they see Jesus. We know that they instinctively know who
Jesus is, because they cry out, "Jesus, Son of God, what have we to
do with You?" Then they say something very interesting: "Have
You come here to torment us before the time?" The demons are
saying, "Your arrival will mean our torment. We're not expecting

You. It is not yet time. Have You come to torment us?"

What was it that Jesus came to do to those demons and to those men? He came to free those men from the demons who were possessing them—and for the demons His coming is torment. Blessed Theophylact says in his commentary on this passage: "See the true nature of the demons. It is torment for them when they cannot harm men." In this we see the true nature of our foe.

We are reminded in this text of the battle we must wage every second of every day. It is not a battle against humans. It is not a battle, St. Paul says, against flesh and blood, but against the powers and principalities, against the demons, against spiritual foes. These spiritual foes find joy when they destroy us. They consider it torment when they cannot bring harm to our souls and our bodies.

St. John Chrysostom says about this account, "Look at what the demons did when they were cast out of the men." They entered into the swine, and caused the swine to run violently down to their own death. St. John says that is what the demons want to do to each one of us. They want to cause us to run violently down to our death. He says, "Do not be deceived. You have many foes. Just because you can't see them with your natural eyes does not mean they are not there. Just because you are not aware of them every second of every day does not mean they do not follow you around, because they do. They huddle around you." What they seek is to enter you so that they may cause you to rush violently to your own death.

This is the nature of our spiritual struggle. In 1 Peter 5:8, St. Peter says that our adversary the devil "walks about like a roaring lion, seeking whom he may devour." If we are going to fight the spiritual war, if we are going to live out this Christian life, then we must be aware every second of every day that the demons are there, and that they are looking for just one opening, just one second when we are not paying attention, one look that is not carefully guarded, one thought that we do not bring immediately to the Cross of Christ, one movement of anger, jealousy, or envy in our heart. The demons look for opportunities to destroy us.

We live so often as if the demons are not there. We live carefree lives, as if we did not have spiritual foes, as if we could relax and take a day off. We say, "I don't need to pray today, I prayed yesterday. I don't need to be in church this Sunday, I was in church last Sunday. I don't need to attend this feast, I hit the last feast." "It's okay to watch this movie tonight; I know it's not holy, but I have to relax sometime. What's the big deal, it's just one scene?" "I'll just glance at that web site, I won't spend much time there. What can be the harm in glancing at it?" "I'll just entertain this judgmental thought for a minute—just a minute, so that I can suck some joy out of it. Then for a minute I'll look at my spouse and say, 'You dirty rotten scoundrel, you.' Just for a minute I'll look at my parents and say, 'You don't know what you're doing'—just for a minute, and then I'll let go of it."

This is how we live, and Satan uses every minute we give him. Each of us has experienced this rushing headlong to our own death. It happens so fast. Spiritual falls can happen in an instant. You can be walking along, even praying, then forget for a moment, and find yourself engaged in behavior you thought you would never do. You can be saying things to your wife or husband or parents or children that you thought you would never say, because Satan never sleeps.

The demons never take a day off. It would be nice if they got tired. It would be nice if they needed a lunch break and gave us a little card that said, "We'll be back in an hour," so we could rest. But they don't eat, they don't sleep. They want to destroy us. Make no mistake: the only thing Satan wants is for you to burn in hell with him. The only thing the demons want is to destroy you, to take away your joy, your love, your closeness to God. The demons have had years of experience, and we must be constantly vigilant.

Many of us assume that every thought that comes into our head is our own, and that every thought, because it is ours, is most precious and must be jealously defended. Once we have claimed a thought as our own, then we feel as if somehow we are being contrary to ourselves if we do not act on the basis of it. It might be a judgmental thought, an angry thought, a lustful thought.

But very often those thoughts are suggestions of the evil one.

Satan and the demons are very skillful at suggesting thoughts to us and then leaving so quickly that we don't see that it was the demons who placed those thoughts in our head. They're very skillful at lining up all the facts to prove the thought.

Perhaps a judgmental thought comes in about a coworker, or worse still, about your wife or husband. For a minute you think that they're doing something they shouldn't be doing. And all of a sudden you remember everything that proves what you have thought. You think, "How could I have been so stupid as not to have seen it before?" Why do you think that all of a sudden it is so very clear? It's not because you're so wise, it's because the demons are so clever.

There is a story told of Elder Isadore of the Glinsk Monastery. Satan hated the elder because he was so holy, and tried various ways to destroy him. The life of the saint says, "Then Satan used his most dangerous weapon: slander." We wouldn't think that would be Satan's most dangerous weapon, but it is. He suggested thoughts to the other brothers about Elder Isadore, and the other brothers grabbed those thoughts without examining them and acted on them. They accused Elder Isadore of something he had not done, and he was driven from the monastery. Satan planted the seeds, and the brothers were not vigilant.

The demons consider it torment when they cannot harm us. The demons' goal is to cause us to rush violently to our own death. We must be vigilant. We must wage a war. You say, "How do we defeat the demons when they are so clever?"

For one thing, we know that the demons will use the same attack over and over again. Even after we've figured it out, they will keep using it. It's only after we've convinced them that we're not going to do that thing that they come up with a new attack. Why are they so stubborn? It's because they know we humans are so forgetful. Paul says in 2 Corinthians 2:11, "We are not ignorant of his devices." Some of us have been battling Satan long enough that we should be able to say, "Aha, you're not going to be able to get me on that one this time. You got me before on that one, but I've learned. That's you—it has you written all over it. You're going to have to come up with a new one, because that one is not going to get me any more."

But we forget. We don't pay attention to our spiritual life. When we fall, we confess it and move on without examining what caused our fall. Why did we fall into that trap? What were we thinking? What suggestions came from the evil one? How did it work itself out in our lives, and how can we beat him at the beginning, rather than beating him by confessing in the end? By paying attention; by remembering; by reading the lives of the saints.

Satan doesn't do anything to us that he didn't do to the saints. One of the most important things we learn about in their lives is their struggles with the evil one. Why does the Church tell us about those? Not so that we can look at the saints and say, "Wow, you're great, you beat them!" but so that we can know how Satan is going to attack us. If he attacked the Elder Isadore with slander, then if we're doing right he's going to attack us with slander. And when we're doing wrong, he's going to attack us to become the instrument of slander against someone else.

If you study the lives of the saints you will learn so much about the evil one. Then you apply it to your own life, and you'll say, "Aha, you did that to St. Simeon, and he beat you. That trick got kicked out of the arsenal in AD 330. I'm not going to start it again now." We have to pay attention.

Most importantly, we beat Satan and the demons with the name of Jesus. It's a wonderful image of Satan and the demons in this Gospel passage, where the demons flex their muscles and scream at Jesus, "What have we to do with You? Have You come to torment us before the time?" And Jesus looks at them and says, "Go." And the demons flee. He doesn't argue with them—he doesn't have to. He just says, "Be gone." And they turn their backs and flee as fast as they can.

The name of Jesus is more powerful than any demon. The name of Jesus strikes fear into the heart of Satan and all his minions. That is why the name of Jesus is to be on our lips with every breath. If we center our thoughts on the name of Jesus, then Satan will not get us with any other thoughts. That's why the Fathers say that we descend with our mind into our heart, and we guard our mind with our heart, because the name of Jesus is our protection: "Lord Jesus Christ, Son of God, have mercy on me, a sinner." When Jesus says, "Go," the demons flee.

chapter 32

Beacons of Faith in a Disbelieving World

Sixth Sunday after Pentecost
Matthew 9:1–8

So He got into a boat, crossed over, and came to His own city. Then behold, they brought to Him a paralytic lying on a bed. When Jesus saw their faith, He said to the paralytic, "Son, be of good cheer; your sins are forgiven you." And at once some of the scribes said within themselves, "This Man blasphemes!" But Jesus, knowing their thoughts, said, "Why do you think evil in your hearts? For which is easier, to say, 'Your sins are forgiven you,' or to say, 'Arise and walk'? But that you may know that the Son of Man has power on earth to forgive sins"— then He said to the paralytic, "Arise, take up your bed, and go to your house." And he arose and departed to his house. Now when the multitudes saw it, they marveled and glorified God, who had given such power to men.

Jesus here performed a great miracle: he healed a man who was paralyzed. We know from the accounts in the other Gospels that this man had been paralyzed for quite some time, and that it was not an easy task to bring him to Jesus. The house in which they were gathered was completely full, and the men had to ascend the outside stairs and cut a hole in the roof of the house and lower the paralyzed man down on ropes. It was quite a spectacle, quite a miracle that Jesus performed: a man who was carried by his friends on a mat, lowered through a roof into the house, who after Jesus speaks picks up the mat and puts it on his back and departs to his own home.

Now if I had been there, I would have had a lot to share with my family when I went home that night. I would have been full of stories: "Can you imagine what happened today? It was unbelievable! You've never seen anything like it!" I would have talked a great deal about the friends and their perseverance, and how I wished I had friends like that, and can you imagine the faith of those men who brought him?

I would talk about what it was like for that paralyzed man to lie there on his bed and be lowered into the midst of the house with all those eyes staring at him, and for him to hear those words. What faith it took for him to move when those words were spoken! I would have talked about Jesus, about the miracles that He had performed, and everything that He had been doing and teaching.

We hear at the end of the Gospel reading the words, "and the multitudes glorified God, who had given such power to men." I wonder, with all my talking about the events of the day, if I would have thought to glorify God, who had given such power to men. Would that have been my first reaction? Would I have seen the miracle and immediately said, "Glory be to God for what He has done through this man Jesus!"

I am afraid that my first response would not have been to give thanks, to see God's hand at work. I would have been so focused on what had happened, and on the human beings who were there, that I would have missed what was so obvious to these men, women and children who were raised in the Old Covenant, who had a different perspective than do we who have been raised in this modern secular world.

We've been raised not to see God anywhere. It's okay if you see Him in church, perhaps, as long as when you go out the door you don't take Him with you into the public arena, because it's not God who works out there, it's men. In our schools we teach the history of men (and sometimes women) and what men have done.

We don't dare talk about God when we talk about history. We don't dare say, "In this event we see the hand of God," because we're not allowed to talk about God. If you want to talk about God, do it in church. But when you're in a history class at a secular university, you're only allowed to talk about men.

You and I have been raised to see everyone but God. When we think that it is God, we have been raised to doubt. That skeptical voice comes in the back of your mind and says, "That's just a coincidence. That happens to a lot of people. Don't be foolish and think that it's God. You're reading into it. It didn't really happen." So we talk about men, we talk about events, but so very seldom do we glorify God who has given such power to men.

As Orthodox Christians, we have to fight against the secular worldview. In our souls, we have to recapture the worldview of the ancient Jews and Christians, who looked for God in everything, who saw all the events of history, as complicated as they are, as the outworking of God's dealings with men. They looked at life as an opportunity to give thanks to God, and sought to use everything that happened as an opportunity not to glorify men, but to glorify God "who has given such power to men."

When we don't look for God in the affairs and events of our lives, then our lives become flat and empty. So often people say, "I don't see God working in my life." I usually say to them, "Are you looking for Him? Because God is working in your life." We all experience miracles all the time. We all have been blessed by God in ways that far exceed our ability to understand.

But how many of us have missed what God has done because we weren't looking for God? How many of us have stolen glory from God because we gave the glory to ourselves or to other human beings? How many of us have stolen glory from God by complaining about the things that didn't happen, instead of giving thanks to God for the things that did?

There is a lesson for us, a lesson that all the Fathers teach. Consider the life of St. Leonid of Optina. In all the ups and downs of his life, he always saw God's hand in whatever happened to him. He would be given opportunities and he would write, "God has opened doors and for this I glorify God." He experienced great persecution and he would say, "God is humbling me and for this I glorify God." Wonderful things would happen, and he would say, "For this I glorify God." Terrible things would happen, and he would say, "For this I glorify God." Behind the schemings and plans of humanity,

St. Leonid saw the hand of God. He glorified God for the power that He had given to men.

That is our call. Paul says it: "Rejoice in the Lord always, and again I say rejoice." Paul says in another place: "Give thanks to God in all things." And again: "Therefore it is my aim to glorify God, both in my life and in my death. All I care is that God be glorified." And again: "In whatever you do, whether in word or in deed, do it all for the glory of God" (cf. 1 Cor. 10:31; Eph. 5:20; Phil. 1:20; 4:4).

As Orthodox Christians, we must be different from the world. We must be different from those who do not see God and who refuse to accept Him. We must be men and women of faith, who believe that God is active in the affairs of men, that God cares about us and loves us, that nothing happens that God has not allowed to happen, that God is working all things together for the good of those who love Him, that every good thing comes down from above, from the Father of Lights, in whom there is no alteration, nor shadow of turning.

We must believe it not only when we're in church, but when we're driving our cars, when we're sitting in our offices, when we're preparing our dinners, when we're mowing our grass, when we're on the telephone, when we're typing on the computer. We must be people who sense the presence of God and who look for ways and opportunities to give thanks to God for everything.

This will make you look very foolish in the eyes of the world. I have a tendency to say, "Thank God," for just about everything that happens. I'll be out buying something at the store and someone will say, "It's a beautiful day," and I'll instinctively reply, "Thank God." I can't tell you how many people look at me and snicker, because it's foolish to them. They would never think of saying that. I can see that they're thinking, "Oh, you're one of those who believe, aren't you? You're one of those who believe that the weather is actually caused by God, when we really know from the meteorologists that God has nothing to do with it—it's the currents and the jet streams and all of that. But isn't that nice that you'll say, 'Thank God.'"

We must be willing to be thought foolish by the world, because as God through His Apostle Paul says, "God has chosen the foolish things of the world to put to shame the wise" (1 Cor. 1:27). God has chosen the simple to shame the complex. God has chosen those who believe to shame those without faith.

Within so many in this world, there is a little faith, given to them perhaps by their grandmother, or their mother or father. There is a little faith, but that faith has been beaten up as they have passed through our secular school system. They have been so attacked for that faith that they have pushed it down and they don't even believe, or they're not willing to face their own belief. Just as I have seen people who snicker when I say, "Thank God," so too I have seen people who react very differently: all of a sudden that faith deep in their soul springs up. It is a wonderful thing to see. I say, "Thank God," and instinctively they smile. They say back to me, "Yes, thank God."

We are to be beacons of faith in a world of doubt, because people want to believe, but they are trapped in a world of unbelief. If we are willing to believe and to stand up and speak our words of faith, then like a fly drawn to the light, they will be drawn to faith. At least for an instant, before they retreat into that world of darkness, they, together with us, will glorify God for the great power He has given unto men.

chapter 33

What We Were Made For

Feast of the Transfiguration
Matthew 17:1–9
Now after six days Jesus took Peter, James, and John his brother, led them up on a high mountain by themselves; and He was transfigured before them. His face shone like the sun, and His clothes became as white as the light. And behold, Moses and Elijah appeared to them, talking with Him. Then Peter answered and said to Jesus, "Lord, it is good for us to be here; if You wish, let us make here three tabernacles: one for You, one for Moses, and one for Elijah." While he was still speaking, behold, a bright cloud overshadowed them; and suddenly a voice came out of the cloud, saying, "This is My beloved Son, in whom I am well pleased. Hear Him!" And when the disciples heard it, they fell on their faces and were greatly afraid. But Jesus came and touched them and said, "Arise, and do not be afraid." When they had lifted up their eyes, they saw no one but Jesus only. Now as they came down from the mountain, Jesus commanded them, saying, "Tell the vision to no one until the Son of Man is risen from the dead."

In the meditation for Pentecost I told you about the house I bought with the garage that wasn't hooked up for electricity. It was an old house and I was very excited when we bought it, because we were moving into the country and I was sure that I was going to become a country man. It was in my blood because my grandfather was a farmer, even though I had been raised in the city and thought a big plot of land was a quarter of an acre.

I was excited that the house we were moving into had a coal

furnace. What could be a better way to establish myself as a country man than to shovel coal? No one who lived in the city would do anything like that. Even after we found out the problem with the electricity I was still excited, because that's part of living in the country: nothing works. My grandmother told me that.

I went down in the basement and looked around, and I loved it, because it was very old. I found all these neat things lying around that were just ancient, I knew. I grabbed some of these strange things and cleaned them off and wondered, "What would this be good for?" You can't throw something ancient away, you have to find a use for it.

I came up with wonderful uses: some were flower vases and others were scattered throughout the house. I was so proud of myself because of what I had done and how I was using these ancient things appropriately—until my next-door neighbor came over to see me, good old Bob. Bob was a real country man who had lived in the country all his life. I knew why he was coming over. Some city slicker had moved in next door and he was coming over to tell him how to do things. But I was ready for him; he didn't know that I was country because my grandfather was a farmer.

He came in, and I showed him the house and complained a bit about the electricity, and he complained a bit about his electricity, the kind of thing you do in the country. I said, "Do you want to see our house?" and he said, "Sure, I'd love to." We showed him around, and I brought him into the great room and all of a sudden I heard him laughing. He was laughing and laughing, and I couldn't imagine what was so funny.

I asked him, "What's so funny? I don't get the joke, what is it?" He pointed at the thing that I had found down in the basement and filled with flowers, and he just laughed and laughed. When he finally settled down, I said to him, "What's wrong?" He said, "If you knew what that was supposed to be used for, you would never have it on a windowsill filled with flowers. There's a reason that was in the basement." I was embarrassed, because I had taken a very private piece of furniture and had put it upstairs, cleaned it and put flowers in it. I had misused it, because I didn't know what it was intended to be used for.

If you understand that story about what I found in my basement, then you are ready to understand the meaning of the Transfiguration, because we all have found something that's dirty, something that has cobwebs on it, and it's called our humanity. We found our humanity, our flesh and bones and blood and emotions and all that it means for us to be human. And we wonder what is this to be used for? Why was it given to us? Why was it created in the first place?

There are many answers to this question, most of which come from Satan. For instance, "Your humanity is given to you so that you might have fun. Why do you think God gave you the senses? God gave you the sense of taste so that you can eat and enjoy everything. God gave you the sense of touch so that you can feel fine clothing, silk and such things. God gave you the sense of sight so that you can enjoy the beautiful sights of this world, and the sense of hearing so that you can enjoy the wonderful music and sounds of the world. You are created to enjoy yourself. You are created for pleasure. That is what this humanity is for. It is to serve your lusts and your desires for pleasure."

Sometimes this suggestion comes in very innocent ways: "You were created to listen to opera, to enjoy classical music, to enjoy a fine steak and a nice glass of wine." Sometimes it comes in a less than innocuous way: "You were created to look at pornography and to release your sexual passions however you want them to be released." However it comes to us, that's the message—that this humanity was created for pleasure.

There are other answers, of course: that this humanity was created and given to us so that we might become powerful. Or the American one, that this humanity was given to us so that we might become wealthy and own many things. Or this humanity was given to us so that we might become thoroughly educated.

We are tempted to think that these are true answers. We are tempted to pursue the path of pleasure. We may pursue the path of immoral pleasure, or we may pursue the path of moral pleasure, but it is the same path. We may spend our time trying to make ourselves smarter, and think that is the purpose for our existence. We can even think that the purpose for our existence is the service of humanity, to become involved in projects of serving and feeding the poor and building houses and the like—until we come to the Feast of the Transfiguration.

The Feast of the Transfiguration is like Bob coming into my dining room and laughing. The Feast of the Transfiguration says, "That's what you think that's for? How silly, to think that God gave you this flesh and blood so that you could be filled with pleasure! How silly to think that the whole purpose of this flesh and blood was so that you could make yourself look better! This flesh and blood, this humanity, was given to you so that you might shine with God's light."

We look at the Transfiguration and we see Jesus on the mountain. We see Jesus in His humanity, and His humanity is radiant; it is brighter than the sun, the Gospel writers tell us. Even His clothes shone with brilliance so great that Peter, James, and John had to turn away; they could not stand to look. When we look at Jesus shining on that mount, we see what we were created to do and to be.

The humanity that was radiant on that holy mountain is our humanity. Jesus assumed to Himself everything that it means to be human. We were created to be filled with God, and to shine His light into the world. That is what this humanity is for.

These eyes were not given to me so that I might gaze upon beautiful women. These eyes were given to me so that I might gaze upon the beauty of God. These ears were not given to me just so that I might listen to beautiful music. They were given to me so that I might hear the angelic voices singing the hymn of praise to God.

This nose was not given to me so that I could smell a steak cooking two blocks away. This nose was given to me so that I might smell the myrrh of heaven, so that I might smell the cassia and the beauty of the Most Holy Theotokos.

This mouth was not given to me so that I might explore the wealth of cuisine in this world or learn how to distinguish between a good wine and a bad wine. This mouth was given to me so that I might taste the heavenly bread, so that I might drink of that heavenly wine which is the Body and the Blood of God.

These hands were not given to me so that I might caress the soft things of this world. These hands were given to me so that I might raise them in praise and prayer to God, so that I might receive the bounties of God's love, so that I might fall down and grasp the feet of God, so that I might water those feet with my tears.

That is why we were created. We were created for heaven. We were created to shine with God's light and to illumine all of creation. How far we have fallen from our original purpose! How much time we waste!

When did the Transfiguration take place? What was Jesus doing before He was transfigured? Luke 9:28, 29 says that He went up on the mountain to pray, and as He was praying, He was transfigured before them.

St. Gregory Palamas, in his excellent commentaries on the Transfiguration, says that Jesus did not need to pray to be transfigured, because Jesus was God. In the Transfiguration Jesus didn't change and become something that He wasn't before. Jesus showed His disciples what He had always been.

So St. Gregory Palamas says that we are not told that Jesus prayed because it was necessary for Him. We are told that the Transfiguration took place while He was praying because it is necessary for us. If we wish to see the things of heaven, then we must be men and women who pray. And not just men and women who say five minutes of prayer in the morning and then go on with the rest of our life until we're beat and tired, and then say five minutes of prayer before we fall back into bed. That's not what we mean.

St. Paul says, "Pray without ceasing" (1 Thess. 5:17). Every second of the day must be prayer. You can receive Holy Communion without tasting that the Lord is good, because if you receive Holy Communion without prayer, then your body and soul have not received the grace of God. To taste heavenly food, we must pray. To hear the angels, we must pray. To feel the presence of God and the saints, we must pray. We must work and labor in prayer so that we can fulfill the purpose of our existence.

Prayer is not something we *do*. Prayer is something we *are*. Until we have united the name of Jesus with every breath, so that every movement of our hearts is a movement toward God, then we have not yet begun to pray, and we will not be transfigured. So today we see the purpose of our humanity: to be transfigured with heavenly light. The path is laid before us. How are we transfigured? It is by becoming men and women of prayer—men, women, and children who live to pray and who pray to live.

chapter 34

Living by Faith, Part One

Leavetaking of the Transfiguration
Matthew 14:14–22

And when Jesus went out He saw a great multitude; and He was moved with compassion for them, and healed their sick. When it was evening, His disciples came to Him, saying, "This is a deserted place, and the hour is already late. Send the multitudes away, that they may go into the villages and buy themselves food." But Jesus said to them, "They do not need to go away. You give them something to eat." And they said to Him, "We have here only five loaves and two fish." He said, "Bring them here to Me."

Then He commanded the multitudes to sit down on the grass. And He took the five loaves and the two fish, and looking up to heaven, He blessed and broke and gave the loaves to the disciples; and the disciples gave to the multitudes. So they all ate and were filled, and they took up twelve baskets full of the fragments that remained. Now those who had eaten were about five thousand men, besides women and children.

Immediately Jesus made His disciples get into the boat and go before Him to the other side, while He sent the multitudes away.

This is a good Gospel for those of us who insist on planning ahead for everything. There are some (you might call it the accountant's mentality) who plan for every single emergency. If they are going to take a trip, they have to pack enough for the trip, and enough in case the car breaks down, and enough in case they get stuck, and enough in case there is a hurricane or a tornado.

Of course the irony is that no matter how much you plan, no matter how many possibilities you think of, there is one that you've forgotten. It's that one that happens, and you find yourself unprepared for it. It's Murphy's Law: the thing you forgot is the one thing you need.

This is life. Life is full of unexpected things. I came home from Liturgy one Friday morning, and I was very happy because it had been a beautiful Liturgy. I walked into my kitchen to get a drink of water and felt a drop on my head. I looked up and my ceiling collapsed.

Emergencies happen just when you least expect them. I had not planned at all on taking care of a leaky faucet upstairs and a ceiling that had collapsed that day; I had no time for such things. If that had happened on Monday, I had time. I had a few hours on Monday with nothing planned, but Friday was booked. Yet it was Friday when my ceiling collapsed. We could all tell stories about how the emergencies hit when we are less than prepared.

I'm trying to imagine how the disciples must have felt on that day, when Jesus had departed into the desert to be alone. Jesus and the disciples were tired, it had been a long week of ministry, and finally Jesus said, "Let's go to the desert and we'll spend some time in quiet meditation and prayer. We'll regroup and we can go back into the villages tomorrow." They departed into the desert and all the crowds (five thousand men plus women and children—probably fifteen or twenty thousand people) followed them to their place of retreat.

Now that was emergency enough—you're going off to relax and fifteen thousand people go to relax with you. Something is wrong with that picture. What was worse, from the standpoint of the disciples, was that Jesus didn't say to them what they would have liked Him to say: "Excuse me, but this is My day off. Please read the notices at the door—My office hours are tomorrow morning. You may come early then, but today is My day off and we need to regroup."

But Jesus looked on the crowds and had compassion on them, because they were sheep not having a shepherd. So Jesus began to minister to them. How beautiful that must have been for those crowds—and a bit distressing for the disciples, who we know had not yet embraced the fullness of self-sacrifice and the complete absence of self, which enables one to find joy in ministering to others.

So Jesus ministered all day. He preached to the people, healed their sick, counseled them, and dealt with all who had come. We can see the disciples watching in awe as the Master is moving among them, thousands upon thousands of people gathered in the desert. The disciples begin to notice that the sun is going down. We don't know which one of them was the first to feel the rumbling in the belly, but they realized they hadn't had a thing to eat. They looked and saw fifteen thousand hungry people—and they saw problems. Fifteen thousand hungry mouths to feed—that is a lot of hungry people!

They came to Jesus and said, "Excuse me, Master, but in case You haven't noticed, it's getting dark out here. We're in the desert. They haven't brought McDonald's or Burger King out here yet. And these people haven't had anything to eat all day. Send them away! Send them away, please, so that they can get something to eat. It's hot in the desert and they're famished, and they will surely faint on the way."

Our Lord says to them: "Feed them. If they're hungry, give them something to eat." You can see the disciples thinking, "We hadn't planned for this one. With all due respect again, Master, we have five loaves and two fish. There's twelve of us—that's a third of a loaf apiece, just for us, and a little bit of fish. If we try to take five loaves and two fish and feed fifteen thousand people, we're going to get a crumb that you can't even see. Really, we don't have any food. We didn't prepare for this emergency, remember? It was just us, going off into the desert, for a time of quiet and peace. We came into the desert to fast and pray—we didn't even plan on eating. How can we feed fifteen thousand people?"

I love Our Lord's response. You can sense as you read it that the disciples are thinking, "Now we've got Him. He didn't think about that one. He's going to do what we want, finally! We've nailed Him and there's no answer but to send them away." And instead

Jesus says, "Give Me the five loaves and the two fish."

I'm sure the disciples wondered, "What is He going to do now?" They had seen so much—blind men seeing, deaf men hearing, lame men walking. They had seen Him walk on the water. Now what is He going to do with five loaves and two fish?

Jesus prays. He blesses God. And you know the story: He breaks the loaves and fishes and gives them to the disciples and says, "Now go feed them." This is where the disciples exercised faith, because the Lord did not give them big bushels of bread and say, "Go feed them." He gave them the broken pieces of the loaves and said, "Go feed them." They had been with the Lord enough to know that when Jesus gives you a small piece of bread and says, "Okay, go feed 2,500 people with that piece of bread," you don't argue with Him. You just go and start giving out pieces of bread.

The amazing thing is that as they went that piece of bread and that little bit of fish in their hands grew. When they were done, they had twelve baskets of bread that were left over—one basket for each one of the disciples. And as the Fathers say, even a basket for Judas, in case Judas would see the miracle and repent, and not betray his Lord.

What is the message for us in this Gospel? It's very simple: God can handle any emergency we face. We look at ourselves so often and say, we're not up to this. We haven't saved enough money for us to do this. We haven't gone to enough schools and learned the answers. We haven't struggled enough in the spiritual life to be purified enough to do this. We look at ourselves and we can begin to despair. We think it is too hard for us, it is too much.

We can say to the Lord, "All we have are five loaves and two fish. It's not nearly enough for this emergency." Our Lord says, "Give them to Me, because I am enough for any emergency. My grace is sufficient." Jesus is enough for any emergency we may face.

The Fathers ask, why five loaves? Why not seven, or eight, or two? They say that the answer to this is mystical: there is another lesson that is being taught in this Gospel story which goes to the very heart of our spiritual struggles.

They say that the five loaves represent the five senses: our seeing, hearing, tasting, feeling, and smelling. They represent the sickness that we have—it is through the perverse use of our senses that we are led into sin. Jesus takes those five loaves and performs a miracle with them, and satisfies the needs of thousands. This, the Fathers say, is a promise to us, that Jesus can heal the sickness of our senses and of our passions. Jesus can transform us from being people who are preoccupied with self, who use everything that we have been given in order to feed and serve ourselves, and to make ourselves more important and more comfortable. He can transform us into people who use all our gifts and all our senses to serve others.

This story says that Jesus can meet any emergency we face, whether it be the emergency of a ceiling falling down because of a leak, or a flat tire, or financial distress, or physical ailment. But Jesus can also heal the diseases of our soul.

Jesus is so kind. One of the baskets was given to Judas. Judas's soul was very sick with the sickness of avarice. Judas was always looking out for himself, asking, "What's in it for me?" Judas was given a basket full of bread that came from nothing. The Fathers say that the Lord in His kindness was leading Him to repentance. Our Lord was saying to him, "You don't have to steal. You don't have to be concerned about yourself. You don't have to ask, 'What's in it for me?' I will take care of you. I have delivered you from the bondage of worrying about yourself."

It is the most awful bondage, to worry constantly about ourselves, and what we will eat, and drink, and wear. Jesus says to Judas, "I've delivered you from that bondage. I will take care of you if you seek first the Kingdom of God and His righteousness. I will take care of you if you take care of My sheep, because these are My sheep that have no shepherd, no one to care for them. As you take care of them, I will take care of you."

Of course, that bread that was given to Judas did not become a basket by itself, did it? Jesus didn't give Judas a basket of bread, he gave him a little piece of bread. Judas was supposed to give it away. And in giving it away, he received a basket of bread.

How often do we say to God, "I'll give away what You give to me. You give me more than I need and then I'll start giving away."

God says, "You give away what you have and then I'll take care of what you need."

We don't like that scenario, because it requires faith. To give away when we don't have enough for ourselves—that's stupid. It's foolish. But Jesus asks us to be fools for Christ's sake. What does He say? "Give, and it will be given to you: good measure, pressed down, shaken together, and running over will be put into your bosom. For with the same measure that you use, it will be measured back to you" (Luke 6:38).

On this Leavetaking of the Transfiguration, we are reminded of the glory of Christ, and we are reminded that He is sufficient, and that in Christ we have everything.

chapter 35

Living by Faith, Part Two

Tenth Sunday after Pentecost
Matthew 17:14–23

And when they had come to the multitude, a man came to Him, kneeling down to Him and saying, "Lord, have mercy on my son, for he is an epileptic and suffers severely; for he often falls into the fire and often into the water. So I brought him to Your disciples, but they could not cure him." Then Jesus answered and said, "O faithless and perverse generation, how long shall I be with you? How long shall I bear with you? Bring him here to Me." And Jesus rebuked the demon, and it came out of him; and the child was cured from that very hour.

Then the disciples came to Jesus privately and said, "Why could we not cast it out?" So Jesus said to them, "Because of your unbelief; for assuredly, I say to you, if you have faith as a mustard seed, you will say to this mountain, 'Move from here to there,' and it will move; and nothing will be impossible for you. However, this kind does not go out except by prayer and fasting."

Now while they were staying in Galilee, Jesus said to them, "The Son of Man is about to be betrayed into the hands of men, and they will kill Him, and the third day He will be raised up." And they were exceedingly sorrowful.

This Gospel lesson continues the theme of faith. A man's child is possessed by a demon. This father comes to Jesus and says, "My son is demon-possessed and I brought him to Your disciples, but Your disciples were not able to cast out the demon." Jesus says, "O faithless and perverse generation, how long shall I suffer, how long shall I put up with you?" Those words should speak directly to our hearts.

Our lack of faith is disastrous for us, because without faith we are lost. St. Justin Popovich asked the question, "What is the distinguishing mark of the saints?" Many of us would immediately respond, "Well, it was their asceticism, their labors and their struggles." Others would respond, "It was their miracles and their wonders." Others would probably say, "No, it is their love: their love for God and man is what sets them apart." All these are true, because they were set apart by these things.

But St. Justin says that beyond those, the one thing that sets the saints apart from the rest of us is their faith. They were men and women who believed. That is why they are saints. The rest of us struggle to believe, and that lack of faith keeps us from being united to God. That lack of faith keeps us from experiencing the blessings and the benefits of following after God.

This morning we are reminded that that lack of faith does not hurt only us. In a mysterious way, in a way that should shake the very foundations of our hearts, our lack of faith hurts God. "O faithless generation, how long shall I suffer with you?" Our Lord was pained because the people did not believe. Our Lord was pained because His disciples did not live by faith.

His disciples came and said, "Why is it that we could not cast out the demons?" Our Lord said to them, "Because you do not yet believe. You've been with Me now for two and a half years. You've seen everything I've done. I've worked miracles over and over again. I've done more for you than anyone could ever imagine—and yet, you still do not believe. You still doubt. You still hesitate at that moment of decision, because you do not yet believe."

It is our lack of faith that grieves our Lord. It is our doubts that bring Him pain. He says to us, "What more could I do for you? What greater work could I do than I have already done? I have raised those who are lame and made them walk. I have placed my hands upon those who cannot see and given them sight. I have opened the ears of those who were born deaf. I raised the dead. I Myself have risen from the grave. And I have given you newness of life. Why do you doubt? Why do you not believe?"

Of course we say, "Lord, we believe. We believe every story in the Bible. We believe everything the prophets have written. We believe every word of the Creed. We say it every Liturgy. Lord, we believe!" He says, "Then why are you not willing to live the life of faith?"

Jesus goes on to say to His disciples, "But this kind only comes out through prayer and fasting." We think, "What does that have to do with unbelief? I thought it was because of unbelief that they were unable to cast out the demon. Now He says it is because they did not pray or fast. How are these related?"

Of course the answer is that those who live a life of faith live a life of prayer. If we are not praying people, it is because we are not believing people, because we really have not turned over our life in its entirety to God. If my life is completely given over to God, then everything belongs to Him. I have given up all of my self-will; I no longer look to myself or to those around me to be the answer, but I look to God. Then it would follow that I also talk to God a great deal.

People who have lots of money invested in the stock market, and who have a stockbroker, don't give all of their money to the broker and say, "I'll talk to you a couple years from now." We don't do that, do we? We check up: we look in the paper to see how the stocks are doing, and we call the broker, or e-mail him. We talk to the one who is in control of our money.

If we have given everything over to God, if we have truly given our entire lives to God and we are living by faith, then prayer will be not something we do—prayer will be who we are. When we struggle, our first response will be to talk to God. When we are joyous, our first response will be to thank God. When we are blessed, our first response will be to praise God.

Jesus said that those who live lives of faith are those who fast, those who do not look to the things of this world to give them their satisfaction, to be their joy. Those who look to God are willing to go without the things of this world because their hope is in God.

Look at the reasons people eat—there are many psychologists who have done this. America is the most health-conscious nation in the world and also the most obese. How can this be? It doesn't make sense, because everything in the health literature tells you that obesity is bad for you. Our nation reads more books about health and we do more internet searches and we go to more health clubs and we're more interested in health than anyone else—yet we also weigh more than anyone else.

The psychologists and sociologists say it is because in our culture the reason we eat is not connected to our health. It is connected to our desire for comfort and satisfaction and love. Food has become a drug to most Americans that they take whenever they are suffering. They take this drug whenever they are depressed or angry or even happy. As a culture we are addicted to food, because we look to food to be the source of life.

Those who live by faith in God do not look to food to be their panacea. They do not look to food for comfort; they look to God for comfort. They do not look to food for strength; they look to God for strength. You see, those who live by faith live a life of prayer and fasting. It is easy to say on a Sunday morning, "I believe, I am one of the believers." But if we truly believe on Sunday morning, then we will live lives of faith Monday afternoon and Tuesday afternoon and Thursday morning and Friday night.

Our words mean nothing. Jesus says, "O foolish ones, and slow of heart to believe in all that the prophets have spoken!" (Luke 24:25). Every Jew would have stood up and said, "We believe what the prophets have written! How dare you say we don't believe! We read them in the synagogues, we reverence them, we kiss the scrolls. We spend a lot of time studying them. How dare you say we don't believe them!" Jesus would say, "Then why don't you live the manner of life they prescribe? You don't believe unless you live on the basis of what you say you believe."

Now why is faith so hard for us? Of course there are many answers to this. St. Poemen was one of the greatest of the monastic elders. One-seventh of all the sayings of the Desert Fathers come from him. He said, "To throw yourself before God, not to measure your progress, to leave behind all self-will: these are the instruments for the work of the soul." Why is it that we don't believe? It is because we don't throw ourselves before God. Why is it that we don't believe? It's because we are really more interested in ourselves than anyone else. We start on the spiritual journey and we begin immediately to take our eyes off of God to see how far we've come. We want to judge our progress.

Why don't we believe in God? It is because we are self-willed, because we want to do what we want to do. We want to be the ones to figure out what is right and what is best for us. The opposite of faith is self will. We cannot believe if we trust ourselves. If you think that you're smart and you can figure things out and find the answers and that you're pretty good at this, then you cannot have faith in God, because as St. Poemen says, the first step to faith is doubt in oneself.

St. Poemen also says, "When self-will and ease become habitual, they overthrow a man." When self-will and ease become habits, then we will have no faith. When we look for the easy life, when we settle into a routine and do not allow ourselves to be pushed beyond that routine, then there is no way for us to have faith, because our life has become predictable and habitually easy. We can fool ourselves when we have easy lives into thinking that we have faith, but we have no real faith because there is nothing that we are trusting God for.

This is probably why the Fathers, all of them, say that in the last days, which are the days right now, it will be more difficult for a Christian to believe than it was in the days of the Desert Fathers for a Christian to go months without food. Now I don't know about you, but I've never tried to go months without food. I've gone seventy-two hours without food, and that's about as much as I can do.

Yet the Fathers say that it will be more difficult for us to believe than it was for them to go months without food. Why? It's because ease has become habitual for us. We don't need God in our lives any more because we've structured them to create a life in which we can take care of everything ourselves. So we are very weak, and we bring pain to our God because we choose the weakness of ease over the struggle of faith.

Father Seraphim Rose, toward the end of his life, had been

traveling and speaking to young people and had seen what was happening in our culture. In a moment of despair he said, "I believe that there are some in our world who can never be saved because their lives have been so easy, because things have been handed to them so many times, and they have had to work for so little that they will never be able to struggle. They will never be able to believe."

Of course he was wrong, because everyone can be saved. But I know the despair that fueled those words, because if we have lives of ease we cannot believe. If we raise our children so that everything is given to them and they don't have to work for anything, if we raise our children so that there is no struggle, then our children will not know how to believe.

To believe, we must abandon our self-centeredness and our desire for ease. We must strike out into the unknown with no guarantees, strike out into that horizon in which we will struggle so that we can learn what the saints learned: that the key to our relationship with God, the key to our purification and illumination and deification, is faith.

As St. John said, "This is the victory that has overcome the world—our faith" (1 John 5:4).